The Complete
BOOK of BEADS

The Complete
BOOK of BEADS

JANET COLES &
ROBERT BUDWIG

DORLING KINDERSLEY · LONDON

A DORLING KINDERSLEY BOOK

To Martino
for his great encouragement
and Fiona, Amanda and Jill
for their enthusiasm

Editor
Susannah Marriott

Art editor
Tina Vaughan

Managing editor
Daphne Razazan

Photography
Andreas von Einsiedel

First published in Great Britain in 1990
by Dorling Kindersley Limited,
9 Henrietta Street, London WC2E 8PS

British Library Cataloguing in Publication Data
Coles, Janet
The complete book of beads
1. Beadwork
I. Title II. Budwig, Robert
746.5
ISBN 0-86318-437-5

Colour reproduction by la Cromolito, Italy
Printed and bound in Italy by Arnoldo Mondadori, Verona

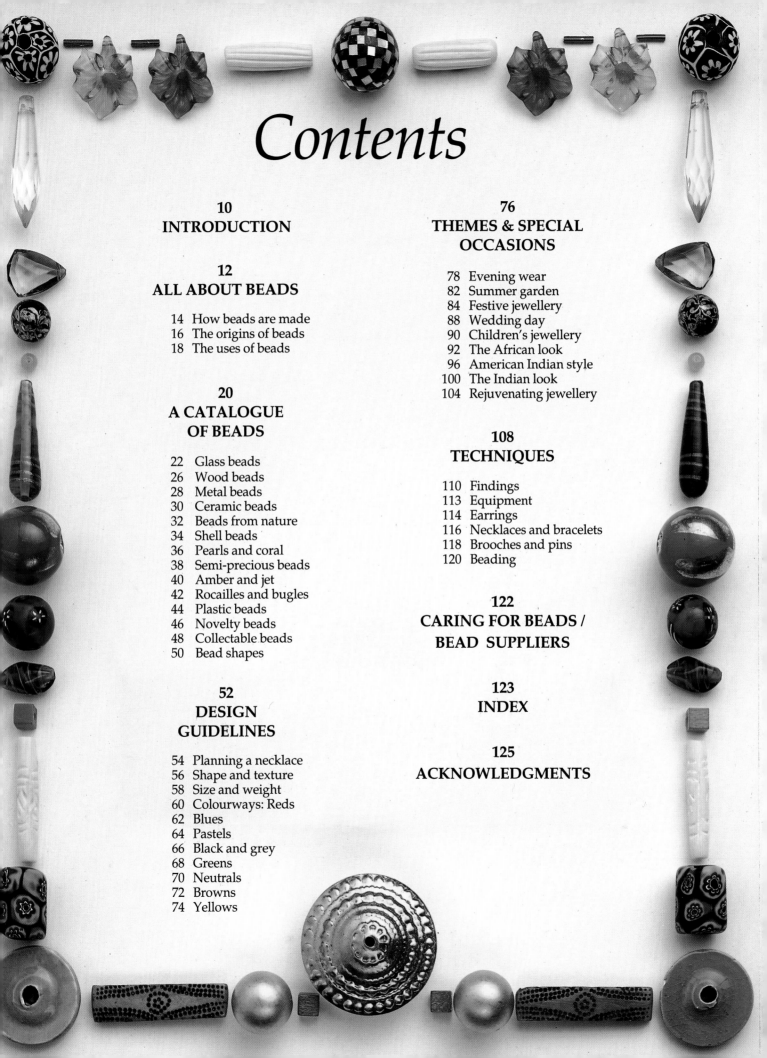

Contents

Introduction

I first discovered beads quite by accident when strolling through Paris one summer with my family. Lagging behind with one of my young daughters, I saw the most beautiful shop window. Lit with sparkling spotlights, gloriously coloured glass beads in the shape of fruit and flowers shone and twinkled in exotic jewellery before our eyes, inviting us to step inside. There, in a small boutique, a crowd of people were picking items from jars, baskets, boxes and containers. They were sitting down to make their own jewellery in the shop and wearing the results as they left.

We were immediately captivated and spent a small fortune before we rejoined the rest of the family. I was selling toys at that time and thought that I could put together a collection of simple wooden beads to add to my toy range. I produced a small mail order bead catalogue which marked the beginning of my business and then started to look round for more bead suppliers.

Before realizing it, I had embarked on something which became more fascinating the further I progressed. I began to learn about bead traditions that stretched far back into history, I explored the secret world of bead manufacturers who have always guarded their techniques with jealousy. In the turbulent 13th and 14th centuries, when the Venetian Doges monopolized world glass making, the death penalty was imposed on bead makers who left the island of Murano with trade secrets.

I discovered that beads were not just cheap plastic items, nor the strings of natural ethnic materials so popular in the 1960s. I learnt that beads have been fashioned since earliest civilization, have been worn as adornment and to guard against evil, were found in ancient tombs, and yet modern beads are still the height of fashion, included in designer wear by top couturiers and changing in style each season.

I realized that beads made at one end of the spectrum by craftsmen in remote villages from natural materials, and at the other in huge factories producing thousands of millions of beads each year, are strung to create jewellery which is worn by people in all corners of the globe.

As my bead selling and jewellery making business grew I started to exhibit at many trade fairs and it was at one of these that I met Robert Budwig. Being interested in presentation and design, Robert started to help me put together my mail order catalogues, first suggesting some colour schemes, then moving on to present colour collections. He was initially involved in the design, photography and production of the catalogue, and his interest in beads grew as he discovered the amazing variety available. Robert's part in the production of this book has been a never-ending search for beads and beautiful objects to enhance the layouts and create just the right atmosphere. We have both discovered a great deal about beads as we have gone along.

The idea for this book came from the numerous enquiries that I receive all the time from my customers asking how to make up and produce a professional finish to bead jewellery. We hope the book will answer these needs, combining both the practicality of jewellery making with colourful, inspirational ideas for necklaces, bracelets, earrings and brooches using beads from many sources.

We hope to interest you in the beads themselves, which are extremely collectable 'small handfuls of history', explaining what beads are made from, where and how they are crafted and exploring the traditions and superstitions which surround each bead. We aim to help you create jewellery by putting colour and shape together to make your own unique style.

We hope your enthusiasm for beads will be fired and that your practical skills will grow when you realize just how simple jewellery making techniques are. I have learnt a great deal through trial and error and there are no hard and fast rules: if the beads hang correctly and you like the style, let that be your guide.

Old broken beads need no longer lie forgotten at the bottom of a drawer. With the addition of a few new beads and a quick re-stringing they will be as good as new and will probably look better than ever. Now you can lengthen or shorten a favourite necklace or convert a brooch into earrings. Above all we hope in this book to introduce you to the joy of combining craft with fashion. Your handiwork could result in a necklace containing beads from China, Italy, the Philippines, Germany and India, drawing on the skills of traditional craftsmen from a variety of different cultures; a necklace that can be both appreciated as a collector's item and worn as a piece of jewellery.

All about beads

The fascinating story of beads spans the globe, present in all cultures and at all times throughout history. This section explores how beads are made by craftsmen the world over, looks at the areas from which they originate and examines how beads are used, not only in adornment, but as talismans, as a form of money, and as a show of wealth and power.

How beads are made

Bead making has been a highly valued skill throughout the world from earliest times. In Ancient Egypt bead making was divided into specialist guilds according to the materials and techniques used, and a similar system is at work in modern India. Techniques invented by the Egyptians and Romans are still in use today and many skills have been shrouded in secrecy for centuries: the death penalty was even incurred for divulging trade secrets in Renaissance Venice. Today in Jablonec, the bead centre of Czechoslovakia, the export of beads is severely rationed, despite high demand, because in a typical factory there are only 80 skilled workers capable of producing 240 pieces each every day.

HAND-WORKED BEADS

Early beads were made from substances used for other purposes: bones from hunted animals and offcuts of stone tools. The rough carving and flaking techniques derived from making other implements. Many beads today are handmade, from sea shells cut and polished on Pacific beaches, to porcelain beads designed specially for the European fashion market.

PIERCING BEADS

Once shaped, a bead is pierced to make the hole. A cone-shaped hole, drilled in from both sides, is a sign of great age often seen in Pre-Columbian beads. Hand-wound glass beads are constructed around a metal wire which when removed leaves a hole, as shown in the millefiori beads below. The hole in drawn and blown glass beads is an air bubble, and modern metal, stone, plastic and wood beads are pierced from one side with an electric or laser drill.

Large flat beads roughly carved from bone.

Each of these Pre-Columbian beads is a lizard egg drilled with a hole. From South America, the beads were buried in clay pots with their owners and their gold jewellery. Treasure seekers would dig down and steal the gold, leaving the less precious beads.

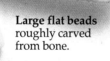

HANDMADE MILLEFIORI BEADS

Complex millefiori or mosaic work developed during the first millennium BC. The bead maker twists a piece of copper wire in the left hand and a glass rod in the right in front of a small furnace (left).

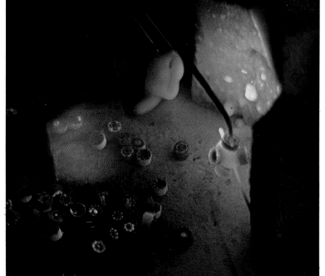

When the glass reaches the right point she takes the rod to one side, leaving the molten base bead on the copper wire.

With tweezers she picks up slices of millefiori cane and places them onto the molten bead.

She continues turning the bead in front of the heat and the canes melt and fuse together.

MASS PRODUCTION

The advent of cheap materials such as glass allowed everyone to wear beads. The Renaissance saw a great increase in mass production for export and today thousands of wooden beads are turned on lathes each hour. The invention of moulding produced the perfectly spherical identical bead, easily recognized by a tell-tale seam between the poles or around the girth. In 1895 Daniel Swarovski invented an automatic process for cutting quantities of quality glass beads. Even today the method is so guarded that workers do not have access to different parts of the factory.

FINISHING

Once shaped most beads are tumbled in a revolving cask to remove the moulded seam and smooth or add polish. Substances added to the cask produce different effects: garnet paper or glasspaper polishes wood, leather gives a soft shine to plastic. The concentric layers of coloured glass in multi-tone beads are rubbed away in different quantities during tumbling to give a two or three tone effect. Finishes, from frosting or lustring to a coating of iridescence, enhance plain beads and are often added during tumbling.

The largest jewellery stone in the world, Swarovski's Superbrilliant is shown here at its full size of 230.5 mm in height and 310 mm in diameter.

Different finishes are applied to plain glass, wood or plastic beads.

Taking the bead away from the heat, she places it in a round mould where it is pressed to give it its final shape.

The pressed bead is left in a cooling oven for 24 hours, then immersed in an acid bath to free the wire and give a good edge to the hole.

COLOUR

Colour is either part of the bead's material (natural or artificial) or is added after the bead has been made. Oxides are mixed into glass and into the glazes applied to ceramic beads. The grain, colouring and origin of wood is often so disguised by varnishing or staining that even an expert cannot distinguish it. Precious stones are dyed or heat treated to enhance the colour. Porous tiger coral, for example, is tinted red with a resin and re-named apple coral.

Beads coloured with oxides, glazes, varnishes and paint.

The origins of beads

Beads have been made on all continents since they first appeared over 40,000 years ago. Initially using local materials, many regions developed specific bead designs and techniques. These spread during times of migration such as under the Roman Empire, with the 'discovery' of new continents by explorers including Marco Polo, and through trading, especially from the 15th century onwards when the world was flooded with European beads. Because of the movement of beads and techniques, the exact origins of a bead and the routes on which it may have travelled can be difficult to trace.

THE AMERICAS

South and Central America have long, sophisticated bead making traditions. North America's native beads, made from materials such as quill and wampum, were replaced by imported European beads when the continent was colonized.

North America Beads were introduced to the Americas by traders and explorers such as Columbus, whose first act on landing in 1492 was to offer beads to the Arawak Indians. Featured in Indian beadwork are rocailles and bugles, turquoise, coral and silver. True freshwater pearls are found in the Mississippi River basin.

EUROPE

Bead making, present in France since 38,000BC, flourished with the Romans, Byzantines and Vikings.

Northern Europe British Whitby jet beads, exported since the Roman occupation, were most popular in the Victorian era. Today top quality beads are made from local woods and porcelain. Amber is native to the Baltic coast. Indistinguishable from Venetian glass, many beads were made in Amsterdam circa 1550 - 1750 and imported into Africa and North America.

France In Oyonnax, southern France, the plastic bead trade replaced the 19th-century horn industry. **Greece** produces silver filigree, worry beads and colourful decorated ceramics.

English import Venetian beads from 1800

French import Venetian beads 1600 - 1800

European plastic beads to Africa from 1900

English import Venetian and Bohemian beads from 1600

Dutch glass to Africa from 1600

Venetian beads to Africa from 1500

Spanish import Venetian glass from 1492

Gold to Europe from 1500

Gold to Europe from 1700

Venetian beads to Africa from 1500

Ivory to Europe from 1500

Silver to Europe from 1500

Gold to Europe from 1500

South America Ancient beads from the Pre-Columbian era (before the arrival of Columbus) are highly prized: jade beads from the Mayas and the Olmecs, rock crystal from the Tairona people and gold. Today in parts of Peru intricate ceramic beads are handmade, then glazed and decorated, often incorporating Aztec or Mayan designs, and in Ecuador bright gold glass beads are popular worn in long strings. The South American tropical rain forests provide the raw materials for many expensive wooden beads, including rosewood and kingwood, mahogany and tulipwood.

AFRICA

Glass beads, first developed by the Ancient Egyptians, were brought to Africa from India in about 200BC by Arab traders and called 'trade wind' beads. After 1680 quantities of European glass beads reached the continent.

Italy The Roman glass industry evolved into a bead centre on the Venetian island Murano, which dominated the world bead trade from the Renaissance. Millefiori, chevron, seed beads and decorated lampwork typify the tradition. The export trade in glass bars explains the similarity between beads from different countries. Coral has been carved for centuries in Naples.

Central Europe Bohemia and Moravia (today belonging to Czechoslovakia) is a glass bead region of reknown, formerly famous for garnet cutting. The area was settled in the 14th century by Venetians fleeing the Doges. Now the state-run consortium based in the bead centre Jablonec specializes in producing cheap cut crystal and lampwork glass beads. Neu Gablonz in

Bavaria is the chief site of the European fashion jewellery industry. Refugee Sudetan German and Jewish glass bead makers, metal workers, cutters and polishers from Jablonec set up in business there after 1945. Agents collect the beads from outworkers, and rocailles, cut glass and pressed beads are also made in large factories. Wattens in the Austrian Tyrol is home to Swarovski crystal beads.

JAPAN
Japan is the centre of the pearl industry and, while it lacks the tradition of the European bead trade, creates fine lampwork. **Japanese** mass-produced beads include fine quality decorated lampwork, plastic beads in many colours and finishes and decals in the Venetian style. Japan invented the commercial cultured pearl in the early 20th century and now produces 70 % of the world's supply. Japan also exports coral, top quality porcelain, highly-sculpted *ojime* beads and rocailles and bugles.

CHINA
Made since the Bronze Age, Chinese beads have been traded worldwide.

The Chinese silk routes were in use from 200BC to AD1000, exchanging local goods for silver, jade and coral. The Ming dynasty made cloisonné work, and blue and white porcelain dates from the 8th century. Jade (nephrite) from rivers in Khotan, central Asia, has been worn since Neolithic times in China. Many freshwater pearls are Chinese.

THE FAR EAST
Beads mass-made in factories cheaply copy those from India and Europe. **Korea** Factories make many stamped sheet metal beads.

The Philippines The centre of a thriving jewellery industry, the Philippines produces beads made in shell, horn and bone. The bead maker, paid a meagre amount, works from home and intermediaries deliver raw materials and collect the beads weekly. Various types of coral are fished off the coast and mother-of-pearl is carved or cut and inlaid as a decoration on beads. **Java** The rudraksha nut is used in Hindu prayer beads.

European glass beads to Asia from 1900

Russia exports Chinese and European glass beads to the Americas 1780 - 1800

Glass beads, coral and jade to China on silk routes

Indian glass, agate, carnelian to Asia from 100

Burmese amber, jade to Asia from 700

Japanese pearls and glass to West from 1900

Mediterranean coral to Asia from 1100

European glass to India from 1800

Chinese glass to Africa via India from 1800

African ivory and gold to India

Indian glass, carnelian and agate to Africa from 200

European glass to Africa from 1800

African seeds, nuts and beans create cheap jewellery. Carved bone beads have been made for centuries, as have beads made by hammering sheet metal, drawing metal into fine wire and lost wax casting. Recycled metal or glass beads are popular and powder glass beads, first made in the 16th century, are native to Africa.

INDIA Beaded jewellery plays a great part in Indian life, worn in precious materials or cheap imitations. **India** imported European beads in earlier centuries, but now

produces vast amounts of well-executed beads in metal, especially low quality silver, lampwork and wound glass, and wood for a fraction of the cost of Venetian and Czech beads. India's natural supplies of semi-precious stones, such as quartz, have been highly valued and traded for centuries.

The uses of beads

Although our clothes have modified greatly over the centuries, the basic concept of a bead has not. A sign of social standing, wealth, beauty and religious reverence, beads have been serving the same functions in many different cultures from earliest times to the modern day.

BEADS AND PRAYER

The word bead derives from the Anglo-Saxon *biddan*, to pray, and *bede*, meaning prayer. Rosaries, a set number of beads for counting prayers, are used by more than half the world's religions: Hinduism, Buddhism, Islam and Roman Catholicism.

A Catholic rosary (right), here in horn, has 150 *ave* beads, representing the number of psalms. Grouped in *decades* of 10, the beads were originally carved from scented rose petal paste or sandalwood.

A Buddhist rosary from Tibet (inset right) incorporates coral and turquoise beads and, like the Hindu rosary, has 108 beads. The tassel bead marks the start and end of the prayer cycle.

PORTABLE WEALTH

Beads are worn both as a show and a form of wealth. King Henry VIII's 98 ounce gold chain represented regal power and could be sold off in times of trouble as each link was worth one unit of currency. Nomadic tribes from the East African Turkana to the Visigoths in 4th to 8th century Europe have worn their wealth in beads to suit a travelling lifestyle. A cowrie shell belt on some Pacific islands is a currency and, like a diamond, increases in value as it changes hands.

STATUS SYMBOLS

Beads and beaded jewellery worn as status symbols can indicate wealth, rank, age, marital status, and station in society. Beads communicate different societies' values especially keenly in Africa, where a Zulu girl's beaded love letter to her sweetheart is a complex language of coloured beads and there are 40 words for different types of Maasai beadwork.

Beaded clothes and jewellery feature significantly in the life of an African Wodaabe girl, and are specially made to show her status at a courtship festival.

A cowrie belt from the Indian state Nagaland where specific colours and styles of beading have complex traditions and meanings.

AMULETS

Beads have played a talismatic role in many cultures. As a source of luck and protection, and to appease spirits, they adorned rich and poor alike either in costly or cheap materials. Beads were scattered on crops in Asia to bring a good harvest, a Filipino wedding cup contains a bead, and each semi-precious stone is said to have therapeutic qualities which pass to the wearer.

Eye beads, made since the Stone Age, are still worn to deflect the evil eye.

BEADS AND TRADING

For centuries beads have been traded for precious commodities by sea or land. From the 15th to the 19th century beads at the forefront of world sea trade were exchanged for gold, ivory, palm oil and even slaves in a profit-making venture bound up in colonization. Thousands of European beads passed into Africa, Asia and the Americas.

Imperial jade
(expensive jadeite) was exchanged on the Chinese silk routes for silks, porcelain and silver.

THE IMPACT OF EUROPEAN BEADS

Beads were not only an exchange rate, but initiated new styles of adornment, and the bright colours and new materials replaced indigenous beads. North American Indians, who previously worked with wampum shell and quill, created a breathtaking variety of intricate beadwork with European beads.

RENAISSANCE ADORNMENT

In the West, where the medieval church frowned on forms of adornment, it was not until the 16th century, when Queen Elizabeth I and other female sovereigns were in power, that bead jewellery was worn by women as well as men to enhance beauty and as a sign of status. From the Renaissance beads were sewn onto clothing, and the embroidery beads, rocailles and bugles, have become a staple of glamorous fashion garments.

19th-century European trade beads bought in Africa. Until 1950 the Zulu people imported 40 tons of beads a year as currency.

MODERN TRENDS IN BEADS

With the advent of a 19th-century middle class market for beads came new materials and techniques, such as steel, cast iron and plastics, enabling more people to wear jewellery. At the end of the 19th century art nouveau introduced a new breed of bead makers. Louis Comfort Tiffany invented luminous antique-style 'fumed' glass; René Lalique used beads and stones for their beauty, not their value. In 1925 art deco produced abstract geometric and Oriental shapes in strong colours and experimented with non-precious materials.

Art deco necklace combining geometric jet with ornate Venetian lampwork beads.

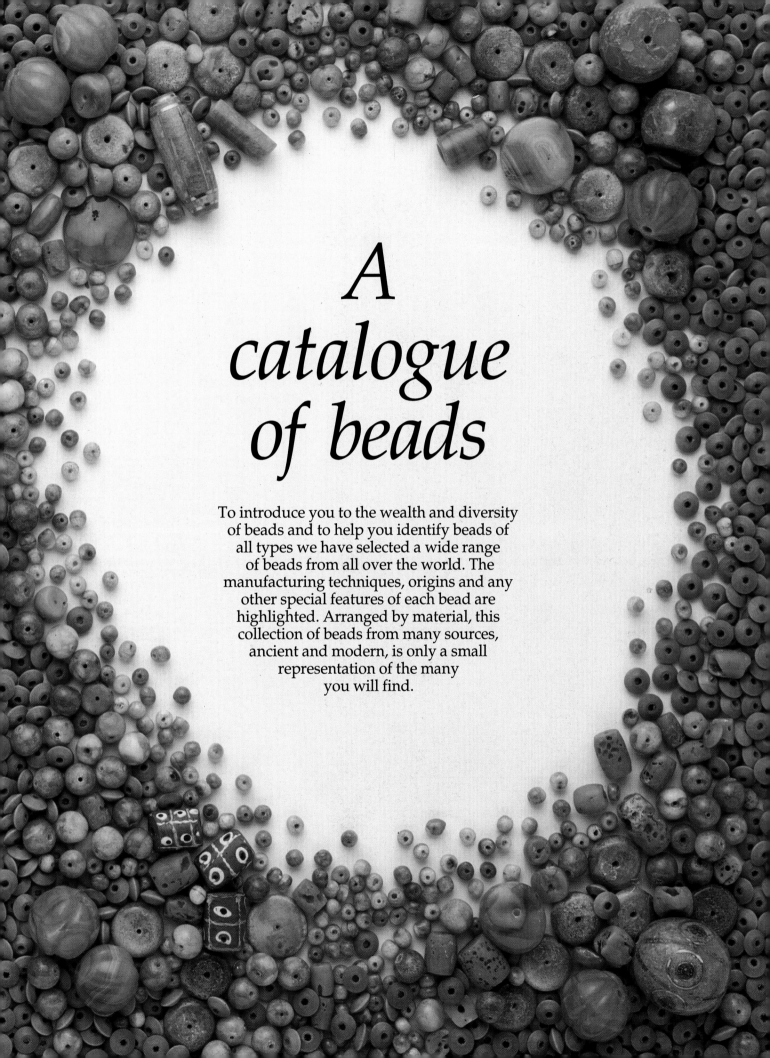

A catalogue of beads

To introduce you to the wealth and diversity of beads and to help you identify beads of all types we have selected a wide range of beads from all over the world. The manufacturing techniques, origins and any other special features of each bead are highlighted. Arranged by material, this collection of beads from many sources, ancient and modern, is only a small representation of the many you will find.

Glass beads

Glass, a mixture of quartz sand, potash or soda, heated with lime, was invented in Egypt about 9,000 years ago. It has been crafted into beads ever since, using techniques invented by the Egyptians and Romans. Glass beads are essential to adornment the world over and the trade is surrounded by secrecy. Glass bead-making techniques are still passed down by word of mouth in Venice, where in 1292 glass makers were moved to the island of Murano and forbidden, on pain of death, to reveal their secrets or emigrate.

OPAQUE GLASS

Additives such as oxides give glass a creamy porcelain or chalk-like consistency, and the opaque colour, which fades as the glass thickens.

WOUND BEADS
Molten glass is wound by hand around a metal wire, the mandrel, following an ancient technique, to create one of the most common types of bead.

Winding traps air bubbles around the stem

Swirl marks and colour variations are common

The hole is large because the bead is wound

LAMPWORK BEADS
Lampwork is so called because molten glass is wound around copper wire which is heated over a lamp.

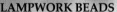

Marbled Venetian lampwork.

Blue and green glass canes used for these small beads are fused together to make two-coloured beads.

Embedded metal

Small beads have a chalky powdered white hole

FANCY BEADS
Lampwork beads are often lavishly decorated.

Foil decoration on the glass core is covered with a translucent glass layer.

Silver foil

Gold foil

Czech foiled triangular bead with twisted edges.

Goldstone decoration uses a form of glass invented in Venice.

Exposure to oxygen through cracks tarnishes the foil

Cane patterns on the outer layer of glass

CANE OF GOLDSTONE
Goldstone, or aventurine, from a Czech glass factory, made with spangles of mica.

Molten cane is painted on the foil

The base bead shows beneath the goldstone coating

Rich Bohemian beads with goldstone and rosebud trims.

Venetian goldstone

Indian lozenge-shaped beads decorated with goldstone bands.

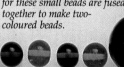

Trail decoration is a skilled art similar to calligraphy: molten canes of coloured glass are trailed over the bead.

Coloured glass spirals

Spiral threads sharply dragged, or combed, one way create a festoon pattern.

Feather design is combed up and down.

Crumb decoration is created by rolling a molten bead in glass chips.

Crumbs feel smooth or knobbly.

Raised eye decoration has adorned Ancient Egyptian, Roman and Islamic beads.

Raised icing-like trails on wound beads are often called Wedding Cake.

MOSAIC BEADS

Mosaic beads are the most ornate type of glass bead. Originating with the Romans and Egyptians, they are built up with segments of glass cane and many of the most beautiful examples are Venetian.

LACE BOBBIN SPANGLES
Ornamental bead spangles traditionally weigh down and identify lace bobbins.

The darker core beneath the exterior pattern

CROSS-SECTION OF MOSAIC GLASS

The pattern, here made from four to six layers of glass, runs throughout the cane.

Millefiori beads Translated from the Italian, millefiori means thousand flowers. A cane fused from different layers of coloured glass resembles tiny flowers in cross-section. Sections of this cane are melted onto the surface of a bead.

Indian millefiori

Cracks show how the different scraps of glass cane flower fit together.

End of Day beads were originally made from oddments of cane left over at the end of a day's work.

A cane is formed from multi-layered glass.

Stripes may be painted on top

Chevron beads Also called the rosetta or star bead, the chevron is the most popular bead in history. Since its invention in 15th-century Venice, more than 100 variations have been made.

The layered glass block is drawn out to a great length, then sectioned into beads.

Beads may be reheated and ground down to display the famous zig-zag of colours.

Chevrons are usually a distinctive blue with white and brick red stripes

A corrugated mould presses points, generally 12, into the surface, then further glass coatings are added

The Venetian and Dutch chevron, the 'aristocrat of beads', was esteemed so highly in Africa that it was worn by only the most important tribal leaders.

Glass beads

The glass bead is infinitely various. Easy to care for, with light-catching properties sparkling at different angles, it has been highly prized since its invention. The art of making glass beads, originally to simulate semi-precious stones, from malachite and lapis lazuli to diamonds, developed with the Ancient Egyptians and Romans, who also originated an enormous variety of other glass beads.

SWAROVSKI GLASS
Daniel Swarovski, born in Bohemia in 1862, developed a machine to cut glass, formerly worked only by hand, to meet growing market demands. He refined the crystal, which imitates rock crystal, to a state of perfect brilliance in his Austrian factory.

Swarovski cut crystals and stones are considered the world's best.

Cube shape   *Drop shape*   *Faceted crystal bead*

Amethyst colour   *Peridot colour*   *Sapphire colour*

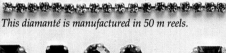
This diamanté is manufactured in 50 m reels.

Strass, developed by Swarovski and also known as diamanté, is lead crystal in a metal setting.

Set stones in a range of colours.   *Rhodium-plated claws secure the stone.*

Light reflects out because foil, a thin piece of metal, is sandwiched between the stone and the back

Cabochons are flat-backed embroidery stones, domed on one side

   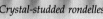
Crystal-studded rondelles

SEMI-PRECIOUS GLASS
Since its invention, glass has been used to imitate gemstones.

Lapis lazuli   *Carnelian*

Turquoise with brown veins   *Turquoise with blue veins*   *Malachite*   *Malachite from Kashgar, China.*

BLOWN GLASS
A blown bead is formed just as a balloon is inflated. The craftsman blows a small piece of molten glass on the end of a glass tube until the bead reaches the right dimensions.

A patterned glass rod is blown into a mould.

Beads blown freehand, rather than into a mould

Molten glass is touched onto the hollow bead while still hot.

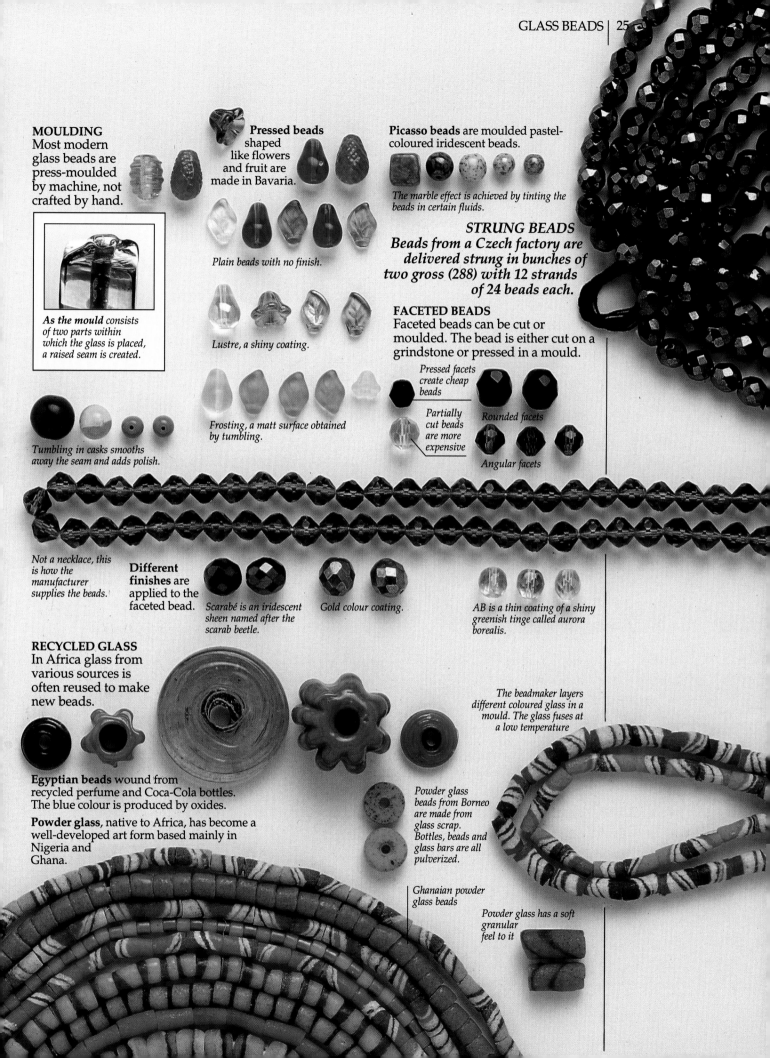

MOULDING
Most modern glass beads are press-moulded by machine, not crafted by hand.

As the mould consists of two parts within which the glass is placed, a raised seam is created.

Tumbling in casks smooths away the seam and adds polish.

Pressed beads shaped like flowers and fruit are made in Bavaria.

Plain beads with no finish.

Lustre, a shiny coating.

Frosting, a matt surface obtained by tumbling.

Picasso beads are moulded pastel-coloured iridescent beads.

The marble effect is achieved by tinting the beads in certain fluids.

STRUNG BEADS
Beads from a Czech factory are delivered strung in bunches of two gross (288) with 12 strands of 24 beads each.

FACETED BEADS
Faceted beads can be cut or moulded. The bead is either cut on a grindstone or pressed in a mould.

Pressed facets create cheap beads

Partially cut beads are more expensive

Rounded facets

Angular facets

Not a necklace, this is how the manufacturer supplies the beads.

Different finishes are applied to the faceted bead.

Scarabé is an iridescent sheen named after the scarab beetle.

Gold colour coating.

AB is a thin coating of a shiny greenish tinge called aurora borealis.

RECYCLED GLASS
In Africa glass from various sources is often reused to make new beads.

Egyptian beads wound from recycled perfume and Coca-Cola bottles. The blue colour is produced by oxides.

Powder glass, native to Africa, has become a well-developed art form based mainly in Nigeria and Ghana.

The beadmaker layers different coloured glass in a mould. The glass fuses at a low temperature

Powder glass beads from Borneo are made from glass scrap. Bottles, beads and glass bars are all pulverized.

Ghanaian powder glass beads

Powder glass has a soft granular feel to it

Wood beads

Wood has been used to craft beads since man's earliest beginnings. Easy to work, warm to the touch, and fragrant, wood lends itself both to incredible creations from the most skilled carver, and plain, simple shapes from the novice. Ranging from purest white to ebony, from solid to light and porous, grained or patterned, wood is infinitely varied in colour and texture. Each wood has its own beauty which is fully explored by craftsmen throughout the world.

LEAVES, BARK AND STEMS
As well as the timber, other parts of a tree are made into beads or incorporated in their decoration.

Banana leaf beads from the Philippines are made by gluing and lacquering leaves onto a basic wood shape.

Stemwood or sapwood from trees like the bamboo or palm is squishy and soft in its green state and easily moulded.

Markings show where the sap has risen

Palm bead

Bamboo is a fast-growing tropical grass. It has a woody-walled stem and makes beads with natural holes.

Cork beads are formed from the thick, porous outer bark of the cork oak tree.

The ridged joints of the bamboo

PINE AND OTHER SOFTWOODS
The product of conifers, softwood has strong markings which make these wooden beads immediately identifiable.

When stained, the markings on pine and other softwood beads show up very clearly.

This natural softwood bead has been expertly carved with 14 sides

Ramin dowel, more familiar to the builder, is drilled to form a chunky bead

TEMPERATE HARDWOODS
The timber of deciduous trees creates beads which are dense and hard because of the slow growth of these trees. Craftsman-made, these beads formed from English woods are tumbled with garnet paper for almost a week to produce the fine finish.

Yew wood log, with the annual growth rings clearly visible, before it is crafted into beads.

Yew wood beads

Holly wood beads

Walnut wood beads

Oak wood beads

TROPICAL HARDWOODS

These beads are made from tropical broadleaved trees. Many tropical hardwood forests are now endangered due to the demand for such wood and the razing of the forest for farming.

Brazilian mahogany

Red mahogany, probably from Honduras.

Tulipwood from Brazil.

FORESTS IN PERIL

Many tropical forests, such as this Brazilian rain forest, are in danger as they are cleared for farming.

Rosewood, so called because when cut it reveals a rosy marking.

Onion bokote: tulipwood, smoothed and polished into chunky discs.

A section through Brazilian tulipwood

Purpleheart from Colombia.

South American kingwood.

Cocobolo from Central America.

Grande pallisander from the West Indies.

DECORATED BEADS

With the addition of paint, inlays or intricate carving, plain wood can be transformed.

Inlaid and applied beads are craftsman-made.

Chunky pieces of metal are set into the wood

Mother-of-pearl inlays

Layered beads from the Philippines made with dowels sandwiched from different woods.

Ribbed beads are scored or gouged using hot rods.

Black staining imitates natural ebony.

Hand-carved Indian ebony beads inlaid with twisted brass wire.

NETSUKE BEADS

An ornamental Japanese carrying case, the netsuke was secured with a carved bead, or ojime. *Over the centuries* ojime *carving became a highly skilled form of sculpture, with mask* ojime *and zodiac creatures such as these most popular.*

Hand-painted wood is decorated with traditional and contemporary Indian designs.

Simple stripes

Carved beads from China are intricately worked, mostly in traditional boxwood.

Completely hollow beads require great skill in carving.

Chinese carved knot.

Marbled effects

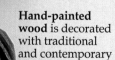

Indian animal motif

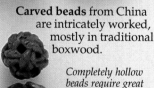

Chinese 'cinnabar' beads.

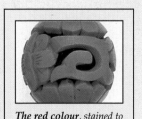

The red colour, stained to appear like the mineral cinnabar, is overlaid on a black wooden bead.

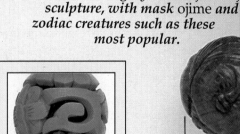

Metal beads

Natural ore minerals and precious metals such as gold, silver and platinum were discovered first 8 - 10,000 years ago. Mixed together, base metals such as copper and tin produced bronze, copper and zinc made brass and these new alloys, so useful for tools, weapons and vessels, were also used for adornment. Where gold work adorned kings and pharaohs, the same techniques were used to craft metal alloys into jewels for ordinary people.

TYPES OF METAL

The four beads on the left are base metal; the four on the right are gold and silver.

STAMPING, HAMMERING AND EMBOSSING

Stamping with a shaped mould cuts out the bead from a metal sheet.

The two stamped halves are soldered together

Hexagonal stamped metal beads from India.

The two halves before soldering

A large hole for threading cord or several strands of leather

Spirals and melon shapes are all made using the stamping method.

Stamped from a flat sheet with punched holes.

Made industrially from perforated sheet.

This bead looks like filigree but is made from raw unplated metal, stamped then riveted in the middle.

Hammering is an ancient technique used to decorate beads.

Tiny hammer marks are beaten into the copper by an Indian craftsman

A high quality finish hammered in an Italian factory.

Woven metalwork from the Philippines.

Embossed metal is stamped by a die with an intaglio pattern (a design carved into the material).

Raised indentations are made by the die striking on the reverse side

NATURAL METAL

The Berbers in Marrakech use locally mined pyrites of mica, an iron sulphide mineral, faceted and set in silver, as in this necklace.

FILIGREE

Filigree is ornamental metalwork and the term derives from the Latin words *filum*, wire, and *granum*, grain or bead.

Fine wire, twisted, plain or plaited, is soldered onto silver

Open filigree, made without a metal foundation

Granulation, tiny grains of metal built up into an ornate pattern, developed in Egypt and Etruria.

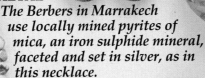

Mass-made gilt-dipped filigree

Usually reserved for precious metal, this superb Turkish filigree is worked in base metal

RECYCLING

Craftsmen in parts of Africa create beads from cast-offs such as melted-down coins, saucepans and car fittings.

Heavy beads with large holes.

Maasai aluminium beads, possibly made from saucepans.

ENAMELLING

Enamel colours are painted onto metal ware.

Cloisonné decoration. Wire-enclosed spaces, *cloisons*, are painted with coloured enamels.

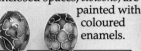

Cells formed on the surface of the bead with thin metal strips are filled in with enamel.

FINISHES

A finish is a coat of quality metal.

Gilt dip is of high quality.

Silver dip coating.

Gilt plating is cheap, but effective.

Silver plating is deposited electrolytically.

Liquid gold when threaded together looks like chain.

Liquid silver is essential to jewellery makers.

Chamba valley enamelwork from the Himalayan foothills is typical of this North Indian region.

Copper finish.

Brass finish.

Nickel plating, used widely in the findings industry.

TRADITIONAL DESIGNS

In many areas of the globe it is impossible to date beads; over the centuries the shapes have not altered.

Yemeni beads probably made in the 1910s by Jewish silversmiths.

Collared bead in the Indian style.

LOST WAX FACE BEAD

Lost wax is an ancient African art form. Carved wax encased in a clay or plaster mould is heated until it runs out of a hole or is 'lost'.

Molten metal is then poured in. It is said that the King of Asante wore such heavy lost wax regalia that he had to rest his arms on the heads of small boys.

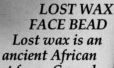

Greek designs in base metal.

Indian silver alloy, not containing enough silver to reach sterling silver quality, is made into a variety of traditional shapes.

Fine silver filigree from Crete.

Far Eastern copies of traditional Indian shapes.

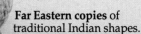

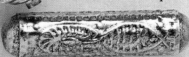

Ceramic beads

Clay is part of the earth's surface which becomes workable once the impurities are removed. Because it can be so easily modelled, decorated and baked hard, it has been used to make ceramic beads in all parts of the world by artisans from all walks of life, and distinctive traditions have evolved over the centuries. Ceramic beads, probably first made when Neolithic man started to mould pots and utensils, now range from simple lumps of baked clay to the finest porcelain worked with extreme skill and incorporating wonderful colour combinations.

TESTING CERAMICS

Unglazed clay, found near the hole on a bead, will stick to the tongue if it is of poor quality. Top quality clay is not porous.

AFRICAN POTTERY BEADS

The simplest clay beads are shaped by rolling between the fingers.

Before the beads are left out in the sun to harden or are baked in a fire, simple patterns are scratched on them with a fingernail.

Decorated with a traditional design, this cubed bead has been signed by the artist and glazed.

ENGLISH CERAMIC BEADS

The best quality clay, as used for many years by English porcelain makers in Stoke-on-Trent, is made into top grade ceramic beads.

Hand-rolled, each shape is press-moulded before a six-hour firing at 1140 °C.

Three coats of glaze are applied by hand before the second firing.

PORCELAIN BEADS

Porcelain is a hard, white, translucent clay, fired at high temperatures.

Hollow lace beads in delicate pink porcelain.

EGYPTIAN PASTE

The Ancient Egyptians first popularized faience or Egyptian paste, an early ceramic. Strands of grass dipped in a liquid mixture of clay, quartz sand and glaze burned away during firing to leave a hole. Faience necklaces such as this are still on sale in the markets of Cairo.

Chinese porcelain beads are hand-decorated in traditional styles, using enamel colours and gilded outlines.

   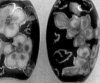

Delicate enamelled colours

The Chinese first used cobalt oxide to produce blue-coloured ceramics in the Tang dynasty (8th century AD), establishing a long and classic blue and white porcelain tradition.

Japan produces the highest quality porcelain beads.

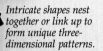

Exquisite beads, individually made by English ceramicist Elizabeth Turrell from black, white or coloured porcelain, are high fired to 1260 °C.

Intricate shapes nest together or link up to form unique three-dimensional patterns.

A final polish gives the smooth finish.

FRENCH CERAMIC BEADS
Handmade in France, these beads are used in top fashion designers' collections.

Marbled with iridescent glazes

Gold brushwork

GREEK DECAL BEADS
Extremely popular hand-rolled beads with a decal design.

Decal decoration features delicate floral patterns

COLOURED BEADS
Metal oxides are used to colour glazes. These simple Greek beads are particularly brightly coloured.

Green is obtained from copper oxide

Iron oxide gives a brownish-green colour

Cobalt oxide produces blue

Lustring, invented in 9th-century Baghdad, is added after the first glaze has been fired, then re-fired in a kiln with a reduced oxygen supply.

Lustrous bronze glaze

CERNIT BEADS
Artist Ann Baxter's designs are made with cernit, a modelling material baked or set in boiling water.

30 available colours are blended to suit a theme, here the colours of the East.

PERUVIAN BEADS
Hand-painted beads from Pisac village in the old Inca heartland are famous all over Peru. Each colour is applied separately to 50 beads held on pins.

Scenes from Peruvian life and landscape.

BEADS FOR THE ALTAR Maiolica beads, earthenware glazed to look opaque, were made in 1920s Italy. Decorated with religious mottoes, the beads were sewn onto altar cloths.

Juan del Cruz workshop in Cuzco produces beads often regarded as the finest in Peru. Costing three times the price of Pisac beads, they are only made to order.

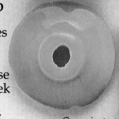

Beads from nature

Perhaps the first beads were derived from animal and vegetable substances. Seeds, berries and stones have been threaded, bone, ivory and horn fashioned into ornaments since early man existed. Sadly, the quest for horns and tusks, often attributed with magical or mystical properties and sought after for Western fashion, has virtually annihilated many species of animal, including the elephant, rhinoceros and walrus. Even today, when we are aware of the environmental issues and importation is banned, illegal poaching and hunting still occur.

SEEDS, NUTS AND BEANS

Vegetation from many parts of the world makes unusual beads.

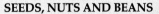

These seeds might sprout if left in a humid, warm atmosphere.

Snake-eye beans from Africa.

Dried watermelon seeds can be threaded with a strong needle.

Acorn cup

From Java, the rudraksha nut is used in Hindu prayer beads.

Assorted African husks and seeds.

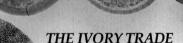

Lucky beans are poisonous, but popular in necklaces from countries as far apart as Venezuela and Malawi.

Named sea pips in Kenya, these seeds float in from the ocean. Varying in size from a small coin to the palm of a hand, the glossy seed is polished by sea salt.

Tropical seeds

IVORY

Ivory comes from the tusks of the elephant, walrus, fossilized mammoth and from the hippopotamus and whale. It has been highly sought after since the Stone Age.

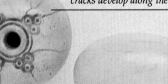

THE IVORY TRADE

Hundreds of species of elephant have been wiped out by illegal hunting to create ivory ornaments and jewellery.

As ivory is organic, in extreme temperatures or humidity, cracks develop along the grain

Carved ivory was popular in the 19th century and Dieppe in France was the centre for European carving until about 1870.

Vegetable ivory, the kernel of the Central American ivory palm, is the modern alternative to ivory.

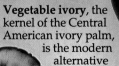
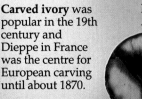

Ivory discolours in age to a yellowish-brown. This bead is about 60 years old.

Graining inside the nut

BONE
Today the bones of specially-bred cattle are used to make beads.

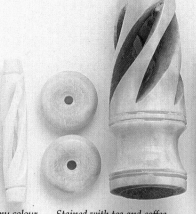

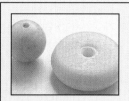

Naturally a creamy colour, bone is bleached pure white.

Stained with tea and coffee, bone takes on a darker hue.

Staining is retained in the relief patterns.

Bone dyed black is very popular.

Ivory, here shown on the left, has a greater sheen than the coarser-grained bone bead on the right.

A camel bone bead from India.

African monkey bone is very coarse.

East African cattle bone carved with a symmetrical eye and line design.

Bone inlaid with wooden wedges from Kenya, possibly made by the Maasai people.

Kenyan mutton bone dyed with a technique similar to batik. Wax painted on the bead before it is dyed does not absorb any colour.

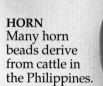

A drilled hippo tooth.

Fish vertebrae have a natural hole

Two vertebrae together form a double bead

HORN
Many horn beads derive from cattle in the Philippines.

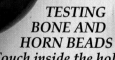

STONE
Non-precious stones have long been used as decoration.

Naturally blackish in colour, horn is bleached and often re-dyed in warm, mellow hues.

Meerschaum, a German word meaning sea foam, is a light porous stone which floats in the sea.

Also known as gypsum, meerschaum is carved and polished with wax.

Granite with its coarse grain makes surprisingly light beads.

TESTING BONE AND HORN BEADS
Touch inside the hole with a heated needle. Real horn and bone smell quite unlike burning plastic.

Red sandstone coated with resin.

Marble, polished to show its distinctive texture.

Shell beads

Ranging in colour from the lustrous abalone to the soft pinks and creams of the conus, sea shells make perfect ornaments, their elegant whorls and fan shapes more beautiful than any man-made design. Shells from animals and vegetable matter have also long been a part of adornment. Used whole, a shell will lend an elegant touch to any necklace design; when it is cut into pieces or fashioned into discs and motifs, the interesting textures and colours blend well with each other.

This modern bead is made from pieces of shell glued together.

SEA SHELLS
Necklaces of shells have been found dating back to the Neolithic Age.

In India the eye shape is thought to ward off the evil eye

Cowries were used from the earliest times in Africa as currency, and in the Egyptian and Maasai cultures were considered to be a fertility symbol.

Mother-of-pearl is the iridescent lining of a shell, usually the Australian pearl oyster.

Mother-of-pearl is carved into motifs and pendants as well as beads.

Mother-of-pearl pieces are painstakingly glued onto a plain bead

Mosaic pieces catch the light at different angles

Inlaid shell bead from the Philippines.

Tiger shell is one of the most decorative sea shells.

Abalone shell is known as paua shell in New Zealand.

Sundial shells, the tropical gastropods, are drilled ready to thread.

These shells have been mounted.

A whole blood conch shell is sliced into sections to reveal the flesh-pink interior.

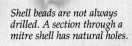

The slices are drilled to hang from earrings or pendant necklaces

Shell beads are not always drilled. A section through a mitre shell has natural holes.

Cassis shell from the Pacific Ocean.

Candy nerite shells are found in waters near the Philippines.

Trochus shell bead made in Taiwan.

Drilled hole for threading

Four shells glued together make a large bead

Polished shell

Conus from the Indian Ocean.

Slicing off the top of the shell creates tiny beads with a natural hole.

Large conus shell.

Antique conus beads.

Conch shell has a long history in adornment around the world.

Conch shell necklace.

Carved conch from a belt decoration found in the mountainous Ladakh region of India.

Highly polished small shells.

Red mitre cut in two and mounted to make a flat bead.

These shells work well glued to earring findings.

Turban shell from the Philippines and Taiwan.

Cut, shaped and stuck together, turban shells are made into beads

Pieces of conus are cut, polished and mounted onto metal for beads and brooches

PRAYER SHELLS
Shell beads are combined with ivory in this Tibetan prayer necklace.

ANIMAL SHELL
Animal eggshells have been made into beads since antiquity. Dinosaur eggshell beads, more than 12,000 years old, have been found in the Gobi desert.

Ostrich eggshell discs from Kenya.

VEGETABLE SHELL
The hard shells of fruit and vegetables can be shaped into beads.

Coconut shell is carved into different-shaped beads.

Coconut shell discs threaded to make a necklace

Pearls & coral

Both coral and pearls are the product of sea creatures. Real pearls, formed within the shell of a mollusc, have been highly valued since antiquity. For centuries their origins were unknown: the Chinese thought pearls were the brains of dragons; Indians believed they came from the clouds. Man has now, with great ingenuity, found ways to copy the pearl, and reproductions range from cultured pearls to a plastic bead with a pearlized coating.

An oyster shell creates a pearl when a foreign body, such as a grain of sand, lodges inside it and is surrounded by layers of nacre, a calcium carbonate substance secreted inside the oyster.

'Orient', the beautiful lustre of a pearl, is made up of many overlapping layers of nacre which diffuse and reflect light.

REAL PEARLS

True pearls or wild pearls are produced by the pearl oyster. The finest are called Oriental Pearls.

These pearls were fished off Kuwait in the last century. They are no longer fished here.

Cultured pearls were perfected commercially in 1896 by Kokichi Mikimoto in Japan. A small mother-of-pearl bead inserted in an oyster is covered by nacre exactly as the true pearl.

No two pearls are the same shape or colour.

The colour of pearls varies with the thickness of the concentric layers of nacre, but colouring agents can be added to enhance the appeal of a pearl.

This pearl fished from Tahitian waters is naturally this colour.

Not naturally black, this pearl is coloured with silver nitrate.

PEARL DIVERS
In the past, poorly-paid divers in Sri Lanka and the Persian Gulf were lowered to great depths on ropes up to 40 times a day to gather oysters from pearl beds under the sea.

Freshwater pearls, often known as Biwa pearls because they came from the now-polluted Lake Biwa in Japan, are today cultured largely in China.

A natural brown or salmon colour, pearls are bleached bright white

Seed pearls are tiny pearls weighing less than 0.016 g. Pearls are usually weighed in grains: one grain equals 0.05 g.

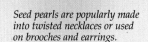

Seed pearls are popularly made into twisted necklaces or used on brooches and earrings.

Australian 'non-nucleated' pearls are so named because tissue from one oyster is inserted into another and disintegrates as the pearl develops.

Baroque pearls are irregularly shaped.

Pearls such as this were once destroyed for being below standard.

Drop pearls or pear-shaped pearls.

Drop pearls are often suspended from a brooch or earring finding.

Bouton or button pearls are rounded on one side and flat on the other.

Bouton pearls are used for earrings, cuff links and buttons.

CARE OF PEARLS

Pearls are easily damaged by perfume and hairsprays. They need oils from the skin, air and light, so wear them often to keep the sheen bright.

Mobe pearls, fished off Tahiti, are sliced and glued to a mother-of-pearl base.

Re-string frequently, knotting between each pearl to prevent chafing and to ensure that the necklace does not break

IMITATION PEARLS

Glass imitation pearls were made as early as the 15th century in France.

Plastic is given a pearlized coating to imitate pearls.

Fake nacre, 'essence d'orient', is made from silvery crystals of fish scales, recently from the herring, and glass beads are sprayed or dipped with up to ten coats.

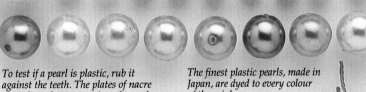

To test if a pearl is plastic, rub it against the teeth. The plates of nacre on real pearls grate against the teeth.

The finest plastic pearls, made in Japan, are dyed to every colour of the rainbow.

CORAL

The skeleton of a sea creature, coral is made of calcium carbonate and grows in warm, shallow waters.

Apple coral is tiger coral with a rosy tint added.

CORAL GROWTH
Coral grows like feathery forests on the sea bed.

Precious coral is hard and easy to carve and polish.

Apple coral and tiger coral have a porous texture

Dark red is popular.

Mediterranean coral is worked using medieval methods.

Few pieces of coral are entirely one shade: most are mottled in colour.

Tiger coral, like all coral, is over-fished and becoming rare.

Semi-precious beads

Semi-precious stones have been crafted into beads since early civilization. Formed when minerals were caught in cooling rock and created veins, they are extracted from the rock by mining. Semi-precious stones have been designated to birth dates, used as amulets and traded as currency as well as being used as adornment in jewellery; and many are believed to have special therapeutic properties which pass to the wearer. Gemstones such as diamonds, emeralds, rubies and sapphires are rarely drilled to make beads as this detracts from their worth. However, some Indian kings and princes did so to highlight their wealth.

QUARTZ
Quartz is a form of silica, one of the most common minerals which form rocks.

Rock crystal is the colourless form of quartz.

The Greeks named rock crystal krystallos, ice, and the Romans thought it was petrified ice.

Amethyst, the purple variety of quartz, derives its name from the Greek 'not drunken': it was worn to prevent inebriation.

The distinctive colour is caused by different quantities of iron impurities and radioactive decay.

Lumps of amethyst are formed into beads on lathes

Amethyst crystals develop with a regular structure

Rose quartz is a cloudy pink colour.

Rich sources of rose quartz are Brazil, Madagascar and India.

Smooth planes are called faces

Tiger's eye is a quartz containing fibres of other minerals.

Yellow flecks are made by light waves reflected by the fibres in the stone

Fibres give the silky lustre

CHALCEDONY
A variety of quartz, chalcedony is very decorative and in its different forms is often used in jewellery making.

The colour of blood, carnelian was revered by the Egyptians as a symbol of life.

Jasper, chalcedony mixed with opal and quartz, appears in many colours.

Yellow jasper

Carnelian, the blood stone, is a form of chalcedony coloured by haematite.

Haematite is an ore mineral with a metallic lustre.

Throughout Asia, carnelian is worn to protect against the evil eye, as in this necklace.

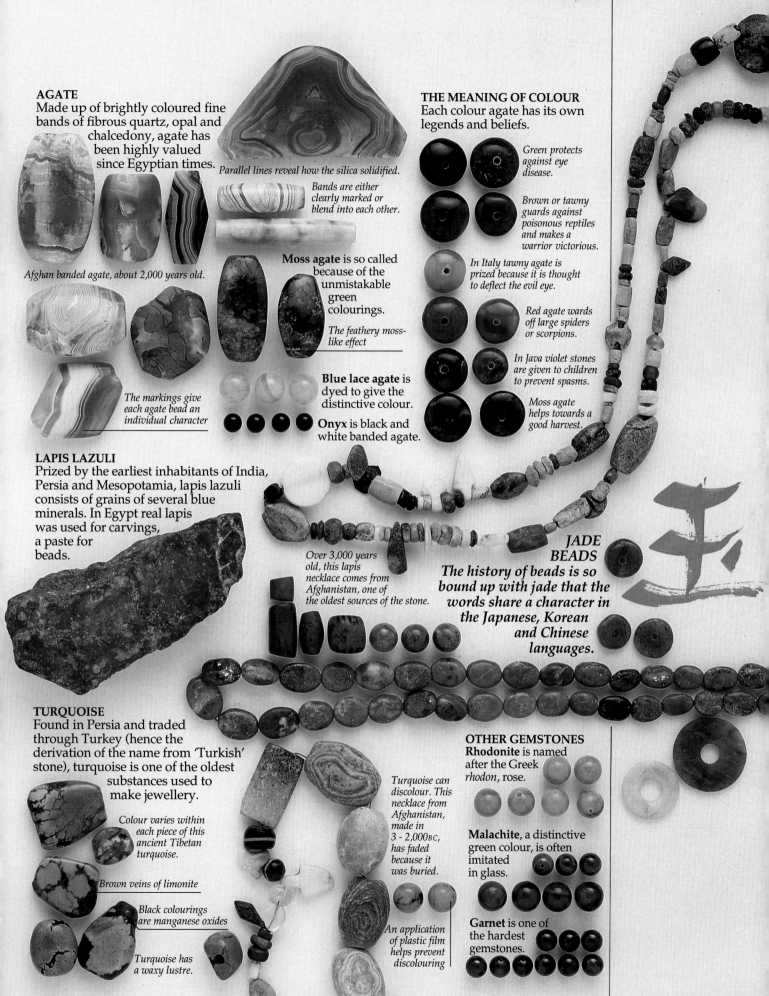

AGATE

Made up of brightly coloured fine bands of fibrous quartz, opal and chalcedony, agate has been highly valued since Egyptian times.

Parallel lines reveal how the silica solidified.

Bands are either clearly marked or blend into each other.

Afghan banded agate, about 2,000 years old.

Moss agate is so called because of the unmistakable green colourings.

The feathery moss-like effect

The markings give each agate bead an individual character

Blue lace agate is dyed to give the distinctive colour.

Onyx is black and white banded agate.

THE MEANING OF COLOUR

Each colour agate has its own legends and beliefs.

Green protects against eye disease.

Brown or tawny guards against poisonous reptiles and makes a warrior victorious.

In Italy tawny agate is prized because it is thought to deflect the evil eye.

Red agate wards off large spiders or scorpions.

In Java violet stones are given to children to prevent spasms.

Moss agate helps towards a good harvest.

LAPIS LAZULI

Prized by the earliest inhabitants of India, Persia and Mesopotamia, lapis lazuli consists of grains of several blue minerals. In Egypt real lapis was used for carvings, a paste for beads.

Over 3,000 years old, this lapis necklace comes from Afghanistan, one of the oldest sources of the stone.

JADE BEADS

The history of beads is so bound up with jade that the words share a character in the Japanese, Korean and Chinese languages.

TURQUOISE

Found in Persia and traded through Turkey (hence the derivation of the name from 'Turkish' stone), turquoise is one of the oldest substances used to make jewellery.

Colour varies within each piece of this ancient Tibetan turquoise.

Brown veins of limonite

Black colourings are manganese oxides

Turquoise has a waxy lustre.

Turquoise can discolour. This necklace from Afghanistan, made in 3 - 2,000 BC, has faded because it was buried.

An application of plastic film helps prevent discolouring

OTHER GEMSTONES

Rhodonite is named after the Greek *rhodon*, rose.

Malachite, a distinctive green colour, is often imitated in glass.

Garnet is one of the hardest gemstones.

Amber and jet

Amber and jet are organic gemstones, derived from the remains of trees fossilized millions of years ago. Among the oldest substances used for adornment, they are surrounded by legend and mystery.

AMBER

A fossilized resin, amber oozed out of damaged trees some 40 - 120 million years ago. It is mined in Burma, Sicily, Romania, Poland and Mexico and has been carved since prehistoric times.

Amber varies in colour from yellow to reddish-black.

Baltic amber, washed up on the shores of the Baltic coast, is also known as sea amber.

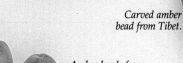

These Baltic amber beads have worn against each other and flattened

Each amber bead is made up of many subtle gradations in colour.

Baltic amber is often the colour of transparent honey.

Red amber is also known as ruby amber.

Beautifully faceted Indian art deco beads in red amber.

Black amber from India is deep red in colour.

Opacity is caused by trapped air bubbles.

Variations in colour are due to other substances: dark particles are usually wood ash.

Amber is soft and warm to the touch. It floats in salty water and if touched with a hot needle, smells fragrant.

Carved amber bead from Tibet.

ELECTRICAL AMBER

The word electricity derives from elektron, ***the Greek for amber. The electrical properties of amber are famed: when rubbed it picks up pieces of paper.***

Amber beads from a nomadic tribe would represent a family's wealth.

EMBALMING AMBER

Amber resin often trapped insects and foliage in its embalming fluid. The scientific examination of such amber has shed new light on the prehistoric flora and fauna.

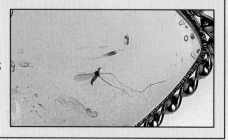

A toggle from the bottom of a string of worry beads from Santorini, Greece.

Ancient amber from Egypt would have been found in a tomb.

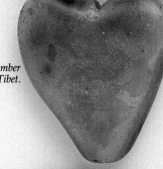

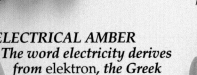

Copal, a semi-fossilized resin, is a cheaper alternative to amber. These Moroccan beads are favoured by the Berber tribes.

The Berber people mix copal with intricate metalwork.

String for hanging the amber from a necklace. Amber is surprisingly light in weight.

Amber beads blend well with carved boxwood.

Amber is believed to have many magical properties and strange fables surround its origin. Greek myths describe it as solidified tears or the essence of sun rays.

JET
A fossilized wood, jet is a hard black variety of lignite or coal formed by pressure, heat and chemical action. Following a rise in the height of the sea millions of years ago, driftwood from pine trees became part of the sea floor where it was fossilized.

Soft jet, from younger strata, is of poorer quality than older hard jet and fractures easily

Raw jet from Iran.

Jet is black, glossy and light.

When polished, jet takes on a brilliant sheen.

Carved Whitby jet, dating from the heyday of jet production.

WHITBY JET
Found principally at the Yorkshire coastal town of Whitby, jet has been traded since the Roman occupation of Britain. Nineteenth-century Whitby thrived on jet, after Queen Victoria popularized jet mourning jewellery for national heroes and her husband Albert.

IMITATION JET
When in the 19th century Whitby was unable to satisfy the enormous demand for jet beads, cheaper substitutes were produced.

French jet is a form of glass now known as French glass.

Tiny beads are threaded onto a base to create a larger jet bead

Bog oak found in the Irish peat bogs is a dark brown wood fossilized to a dull finish.

Enamelled wood from the 1880s also imitated jet cheaply.

The popularity for mourning jewellery continued until the 1880s, when these French jet necklaces (above and below) were made.

Rocailles and bugles

Tiny glass beads in a myriad of colours are known as rocailles and bugles and they are used both in jewellery making and embroidery. Bugles are tubes, and rocailles (a French word meaning little stones) or seed beads are round. A thousand years ago these glass beads were being made in Venice by traditional methods still in use today.

A **long tube** of glass was cut into canes to be made into tiny beads.

MANUFACTURE
Each holding a hollow globe of molten glass, two men would run in opposite directions to draw out a tube at least 90 m (300 ft) long. The tubes were sectioned off to make either rocailles or bugles.

The shape of the glass cane determines the form of both bead and hole.

Two-cut, with facets

Round hole

Square hole

Magatama, a shape invented in Japan with an off-centre hole

CONTERIE
Conterie is the ancient word for glass beads. Derived from the Latin *comptus*, adorned, and the Italian *contare*, to count, it conveys the importance of these tiny beads to trade and decoration worldwide.

Italian rocailles and bugles.

THE WORLD OVER
These European beads have passed through trade into the traditional dress and customs of many cultures throughout the world.

Pound beads is a traditional trade name for rocailles which were once sold by the pound.

A Zulu girl's 'love letter' to her sweetheart is a complex coded message. Coloured rocailles symbolize different emotions: blue represent rejection, the sea and the sky; red may mean passion or eyes red from weeping; while white beads stand for purity and true love.

A mask from Ghana inset with threaded rocailles.

The bullfighter's 'suit of lights' is heavily encrusted with beads.

Zulu bracelets

A North American Indian necklace. It is said that Manhattan was bought with beads.

ROCAILLES

Opaque rocailles are perfect for using in embroidery or bead weaving because of their uniform shape.

Transparent rocailles are available in a range of colours.

Metallic rocailles should not be sewn onto garments that will be washed as the finish may rub off.

Opaline finish gives a smooth, glossy sheen.

Iridescent rocailles are transparent with a delicate lustre.

Lustred rocailles with a metallic sheen.

Pearlized rocailles are produced in very subtle colours.

Silver-lined rocailles are lined with foil.

Frosted, silver-lined rocailles are almost opaque looking.

Iris is a coating of iridescence in many different colours.

Sizing of rocailles is complex and varies between manufacturers. Società Veneziana Conterie in Murano makes 15 different sizes.

STRINGING

Rocailles and bugles are sold strung in bunches. Canada strung contains 1,000 beads strung in ten strings of 100 beads each, while Pari strung has 12 strings of any bead in 25 cm lengths.

BUGLES

Opaque bugles are made from an opaque glass bar.

Transparent bugles are popular for embroidery.

Pearlized effect, also called Ceylon finish.

Satin-finished bugles have a matt surface.

Silver-lined beads reflect back the light.

Iris is made up of many colours.

Sizing Fewer sizes of bugle are made than of rocaille.

A fringed dress from 1930s France.

BEADED DRESS

This French dress, made from the most delicate fabric, is encrusted front and back with an intricate pattern incorporating musical notes, scrolls and waves in gold and silver beads.

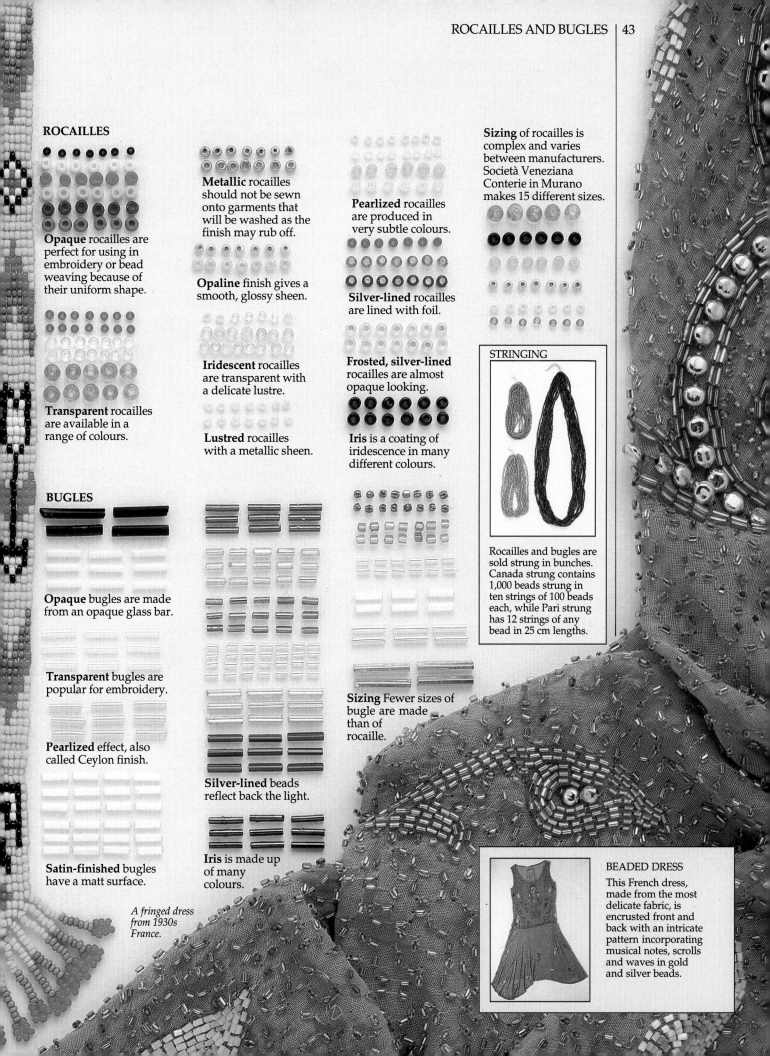

Plastic beads

Plastic is a modern material derived from oil and first produced in Britain in 1855. It is extremely versatile: no other substance can be crafted into so many shapes, nor simulate so many different materials so well. It is the cheapness and the versatility of plastic which are its real strengths. Mass produced, the plastic bead supplies the fickle fashion jewellery market with ever more exotic creations, worn for one season, then discarded for even newer delights.

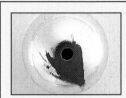

PERSPEX
ICI's name for plexiglass (the word derives from plastic and flexible), Perspex is a tough transparent plastic. Much lighter than glass, Perspex does not splinter.

PLASTIC IMITATIONS
Commercial plastics were originally made to imitate natural materials such as horn, tortoiseshell, coral, wood and ivory, supplies of which were becoming scarce and expensive. Some imitations are so good that it is difficult to distinguish the plastic from the real thing.

Metallized plastic has a shiny finish. The grooves and hollows in the beads are marked out in black.

Beads coated with shiny silver.

The plastic base bead, which is a dark pink colour, can be clearly seen near the hole.

'Antique silver': plastic beads can be made to look like ancient metal.

Marbled clay is copied with a swirled mixture of more than one colour plastic.

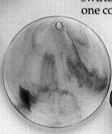

Tortoiseshell plastic is popular now the real substance is no longer acceptable.

Amber was imitated in the early days of plastic by Bakelite.

SPECIAL EFFECTS
As plastic ceased simply to imitate other materials, its own qualities were explored.

Striped beads formed from a bar of striped material like seaside rock.

Mosaic beads made from a plastic bar which contains black granules.

Frosting is a matt finish of powder, which is tumbled onto plexiglass beads in drums.

Stripes are added to this white bead by tumbling.

Stripes will be irregular if the moulding is faulty

Inset beads have small pieces of other materials placed in the plastic during production.

Polystyrene

Silk finish.

Satin finish.

Gold trails

AB coating is a layer of aurora borealis (see page 25).

SHAPES

Plastic is not only made in a rainbow of colours, it is moulded into a wide range of shapes, based on natural or geometric forms.

BAKELITE BEAD

Invented in 1909, Bakelite is a hard thermoset plastic, in the early days used to imitate jet, amber and ivory. This shrimp-coloured Bakelite bead from the 1930s has a punched hole effect.

Extremely cheap, these flower-shaped beads are very popular and are made in a variety of colours.

The moulding is so precise on these beads that the veins stand out.

Faceted heart

Frosted oval beads in delicate shades of pink and blue.

Iridescent grooved ovals

Bunch of grapes beads with metal loops attached.

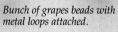

Faceted drop-shaped beads

Frosted melon-shaped beads

Long faceted drops

A 1930s plastic bead is made up from a series of revolving discs.

POP-IT BEADS

Plastic beads became a widespread craze in the 1950s and 1960s when pop-it beads were all the rage.

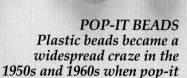

Chandelier

Hexagon with facets

Faceted bicone

Faceted star

The plastic used to make this bead is very brittle.

Novelty beads

From parrots or teddy bears to be worn dangling from the ear to ice cream cones or black cats pinned to a coat lapel, novelty beads are available in a huge range of brightly coloured, eyecatching shapes, made from materials as diverse as wood and plastic. Fantasy takes over and sensible, classic looks are swept aside by fleeting fashions and a sense of fun.

Ebony duck inlaid with mother-of-pearl.

WOODEN SHAPES
Cut from plywood, brightly coloured shapes are hand-painted by an artist so that each piece is unique.

Flat motifs can be drilled or glued onto brooch backs or earring clips.

Necklace with assorted fruit beads.

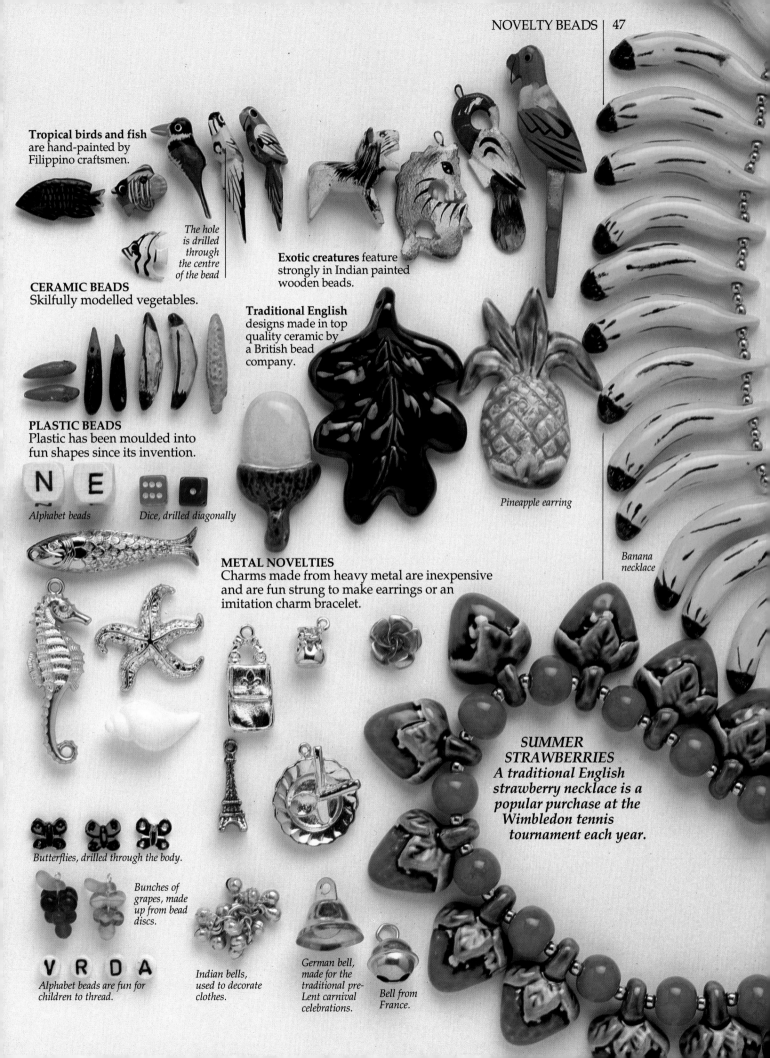

Tropical birds and fish are hand-painted by Filippino craftsmen.

The hole is drilled through the centre of the bead

Exotic creatures feature strongly in Indian painted wooden beads.

CERAMIC BEADS
Skilfully modelled vegetables.

Traditional English designs made in top quality ceramic by a British bead company.

PLASTIC BEADS
Plastic has been moulded into fun shapes since its invention.

Alphabet beads

Dice, drilled diagonally

Pineapple earring

Banana necklace

METAL NOVELTIES
Charms made from heavy metal are inexpensive and are fun strung to make earrings or an imitation charm bracelet.

Butterflies, drilled through the body.

Bunches of grapes, made up from bead discs.

Alphabet beads are fun for children to thread.

Indian bells, used to decorate clothes.

German bell, made for the traditional pre-Lent carnival celebrations.

Bell from France.

SUMMER STRAWBERRIES
A traditional English strawberry necklace is a popular purchase at the Wimbledon tennis tournament each year.

Collectable beads

Certain beads become highly collectable, whether because of their great age, magical qualities, fascinating history, or sheer beauty. Such beads may change hands for great amounts of money, but they can still be discovered in discarded necklaces.

PRE-COLUMBIAN BEADS
Bead making thrived in the sophisticated cultures of South America, long before the arrival of Columbus.

Pre-Columbian beads from Central America.

ROMAN BEADS
One of the great periods of glass making, the Roman era produced and traded complex and beautiful glass beads.

Tairona beads (left) made of rock crystal were carved between AD800 and 1500 in north Colombia. The Tairona people are famed for their stone beads.

Carved soapstone beads.

Although excavated in Mauritania, West Africa, these beads are called Roman because they are of the Roman period.

EYE BEADS
Since Palaeolithic times fear has been linked with the eyes and 'good' eyes created to deflect evil.

Ancient eye beads from Tibet, about 2,000 years old

Glass imitating agate. As soon as glass was invented, eye beads were made.

Stratified eyes made from layers of glass. This Roman glass is from present-day Iran where animals and children still wear eye beads.

Colourful eye beads. Blue is the colour of the 'good' eye.

Face beads are considered more powerful than eye beads in warding off evil.

THE MAGIC AMULET
dZi are torpedo-shaped beads of unknown origins found in Tibet. The line and circle design on these glass reproductions is prized for its protective powers.

Ceramic Japanese double faces.

Pumtek beads from the Himalayas are worth a great deal in their home region.

Bodom beads, revered by the Asante, were once worth seven slaves. Bodom means 'to bark' and the bead is thought to warn its owner by barking in the face of danger.

Yellow powder glass

Always large, Bodom beads are believed to reproduce themselves.

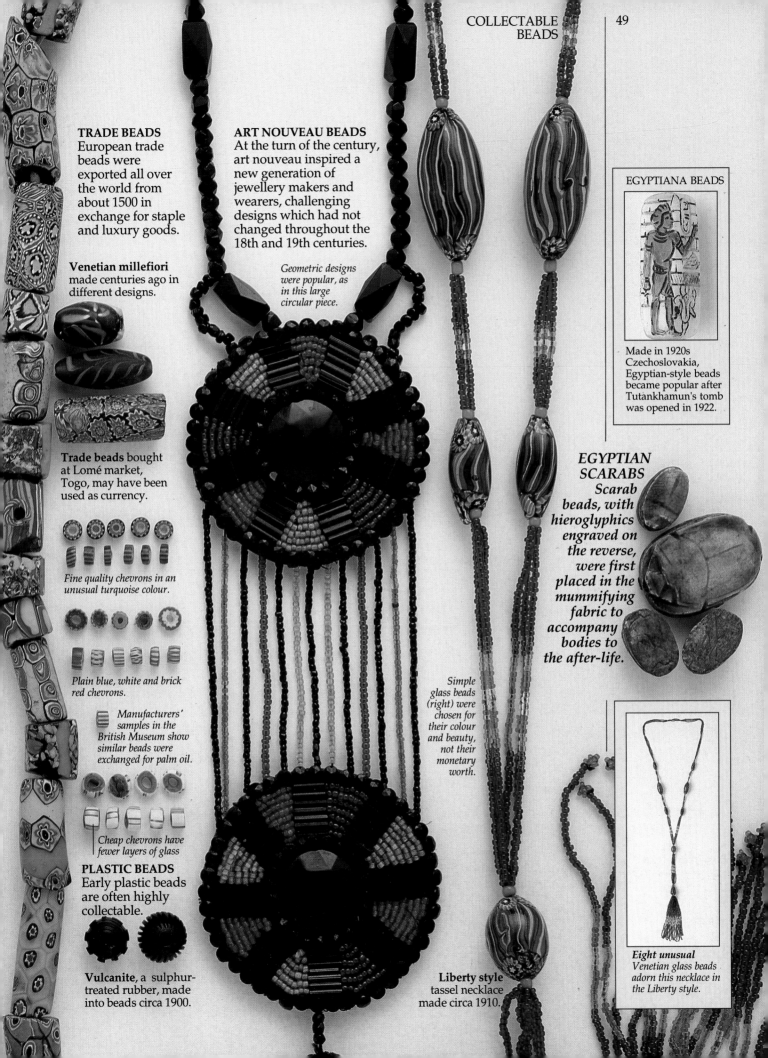

TRADE BEADS
European trade beads were exported all over the world from about 1500 in exchange for staple and luxury goods.

Venetian millefiori made centuries ago in different designs.

Trade beads bought at Lomé market, Togo, may have been used as currency.

Fine quality chevrons in an unusual turquoise colour.

Plain blue, white and brick red chevrons.

Manufacturers' samples in the British Museum show similar beads were exchanged for palm oil.

Cheap chevrons have fewer layers of glass

PLASTIC BEADS
Early plastic beads are often highly collectable.

Vulcanite, a sulphur-treated rubber, made into beads circa 1900.

ART NOUVEAU BEADS
At the turn of the century, art nouveau inspired a new generation of jewellery makers and wearers, challenging designs which had not changed throughout the 18th and 19th centuries.

Geometric designs were popular, as in this large circular piece.

Simple glass beads (right) were chosen for their colour and beauty, not their monetary worth.

Liberty style tassel necklace made circa 1910.

EGYPTIANA BEADS

Made in 1920s Czechoslovakia, Egyptian-style beads became popular after Tutankhamun's tomb was opened in 1922.

EGYPTIAN SCARABS
Scarab beads, with hieroglyphics engraved on the reverse, were first placed in the mummifying fabric to accompany bodies to the after-life.

Eight unusual Venetian glass beads adorn this necklace in the Liberty style.

Bead shapes

Bicone, oblate, ellipsoid: all are names which are recognized equally by the bead enthusiast and the mathematician. Far from being uniformly small round objects, beads are made in a large range of shapes. A selection of the most common shapes is shown below to help the bead collector and jewellery maker identify and choose beads.

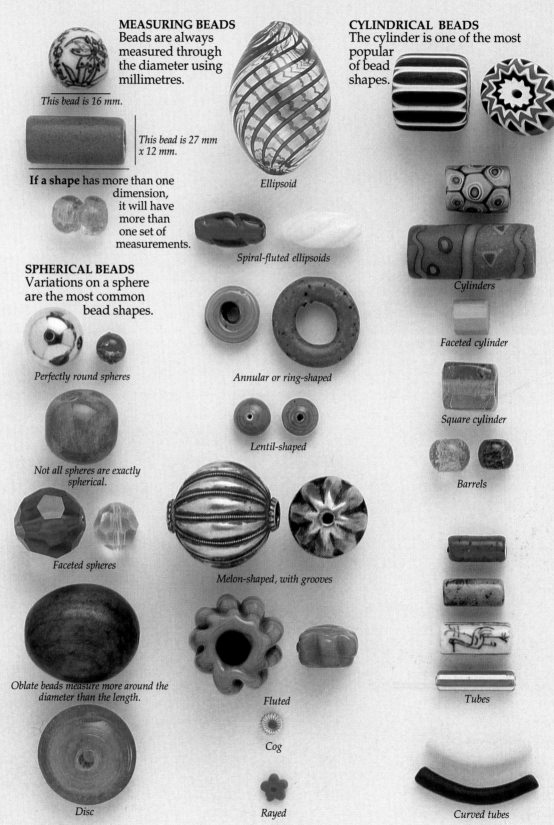

MEASURING BEADS
Beads are always measured through the diameter using millimetres.

This bead is 16 mm.

This bead is 27 mm x 12 mm.

If a shape has more than one dimension, it will have more than one set of measurements.

SPHERICAL BEADS
Variations on a sphere are the most common bead shapes.

Perfectly round spheres

Not all spheres are exactly spherical.

Faceted spheres

Oblate beads measure more around the diameter than the length.

Disc

Ellipsoid

Spiral-fluted ellipsoids

Annular or ring-shaped

Lentil-shaped

Melon-shaped, with grooves

Fluted

Cog

Rayed

CYLINDRICAL BEADS
The cylinder is one of the most popular of bead shapes.

Cylinders

Faceted cylinder

Square cylinder

Barrels

Tubes

Curved tubes

CONES
Cone-shaped beads have been made for centuries.

Cone

Long convex cone, curving into a rounded shape.

Convex cone disc

BICONES
Beads known as bicones form a cone shape at either end.

Bicones

Rounded bicone

Short convex bicone

Truncated bicones: the ends look as if they have been cut off.

Spiral-fluted bicone

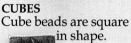

Truncated concave bicone, which curves inwards.

CUBES
Cube beads are square in shape.

Cubes

Cornerless cubes

DROP BEADS
A drop is drilled through the length or the top.

Drop or pendant beads

Pear-shaped

Heart-shaped

OTHER GEOMETRIC SHAPES

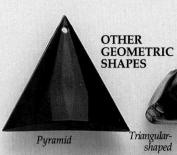

Pyramid *Triangular-shaped*

Hexagonal-shaped

Lozenge or diamond shape

TABULAR BEADS
Tabular beads are flat: the hole is drilled through each bead.

Round tabular

Square tabular

Hexagonal tabular

SEGMENTED BEADS
Some beads have many parts.

Collared beads, with a metal collar around the hole.

Segmented beads

Design guidelines

Now is the time to start choosing the beads
for your own designs. This section shows you
how to plan a necklace, mix beads by shape
and texture, and balance size and weight
to show off each bead to its best advantage.
The following pages feature a feast of colour
ideas to inspire you to keep to one colourway,
or tone and mix shades to enhance each
other. Harmony of colour is the effect
to aim for, with a pleasing and
complementary run of beads.

Planning a necklace

Before you start making a piece of jewellery, you must decide how long it should be, how many beads you require and what type of pattern or structure it will have. In some necklaces the beads are graduated in size, some necklaces have a repeated pattern and others are strung completely randomly. When planning a necklace, it helps to check that the design works by laying out all your beads before starting to thread. Then thread from the centre and add beads on each side. When you are happy with the result, attach the clasp.

CHOOSING THE LENGTH

One of the joys of making your own jewellery is matching the length with your height, your clothes and the occasion. When using these measurements as a guide, allow at least 10 cm extra thread for making knots and attaching clasps.

A rope need not have a clasp; it can be knotted at the ends instead if it is long enough to slip over the head. This rope is twisted.

CALCULATING HOW MANY BEADS YOU NEED

Beads are traditionally measured in millimetres. To work out how many beads you need, measure the length of the sequence (see below) you intend to use and divide this number into the length of the necklace.

These beads range in measurement from 28 mm to 2 mm.

A repeating sequence as seen in the necklace above has no centre and is easy to produce: simply make up a pattern and repeat it a number of times along the length of the necklace.

MAKING A PATTERN

One of the basics of creating necklaces, the art of producing patterns often confuses the novice jewellery maker.

An uneven repeating sequence is an interesting alternative to the usual repeating pattern. The groups on each side of the necklace do not quite correspond, but are all of the same length, giving the necklace an informal appeal.

A centrepiece, formed by a large silver melon-shaped bead, is the main interest of this necklace and the pattern, repeated on each side, builds up from it.

A larger bead, such as this Indian silver melon, works well in the centre of a necklace

A graduated design, with symmetrical pairs of beads panning out in decreasing size towards the clasp, draws the eye to the three main silver beads.

Small tubes of lapis, all slightly different lengths, separate the silver beads in the necklace

A good choker length is about 40 cm.

A necklace usually measures 50 - 60 cm.

A rope can be any length from about 70 cm upwards – long enough to wind more than once around the neck.

A bracelet is about 15 cm long, depending on the size of your wrist.

The simple sequence shown on the right is repeated five times in the necklace below.

6 x 12 mm pearls *2 x 8 mm rondelles* *1 x 4 mm rondelle* *1 x 8 mm bicone*

These measurements add up to 100 mm or 10 cm. Therefore, to make the necklace 50 cm in length, select five times the number of beads in the pattern. One extra bicone has been added to finish off the necklace equally on each side.

The symmetry and rhythm of a repeating pattern make a necklace easy to wear and pleasing to the eye.

To emphasize individual beads, separate them with small spacer beads. Here this shows off the distinctive mottled colourings of the turquoise discs.

VARIATIONS ON A THEME
This selection of large aquamarine plastic and smaller silver beads could not be simpler. The same beads can be strung in completely different ways to create diverse effects.

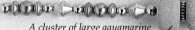

A cluster of large aquamarine beads at the centre

A run-in of small beads at each end for economy and comfort.

Large round beads punctuate a thin strand

Bicones run in a rhythmic repeated sequence

A large plastic bead forms a centrepiece

Small oval beads increase the illusion of length

Shape and texture

Interesting jewellery design often depends on the shape of the beads, their varying textures and finishes and how well they are combined. Shape is as important as colour, and each shape should be well positioned on both a simple necklace and a collector's piece alike. When not put together successfully, beautiful shapes and colours can blur, leaving the viewer confused. Having chosen the style of jewellery that you wish to make, start to search for stunning unusual beads and the invaluable fillers, or spacers, which although insignificant-looking contribute so much to a design.

MIXING DIFFERENT TEXTURES
This bold necklace is so eyecatching because it successfully combines contrasting textures that one would not automatically mix.

COMBINING MATERIALS
Simple stained wooden beads strung together on their own might look rather childlike, but they take on an elegant air when enlivened with rich Venetian glass tubes, plastic pearls and silver brass beads.

MOSTLY WOOD
Retain the wooden beads but leave out the highly shiny plastic pearls and silver bells to make a simple bracelet which matches the Indian-type necklace.

The spherical shape and smooth polish of these plastic beads shows to the full when they are separated by rocailles.

USING SPACER BEADS
To emphasize individual beads, separate them with spacer, or filler, beads.

A bracelet shows how the beads look when strung together without spacer beads.

Plaited cord, which ties at the back of the neck, catches the mood of the necklace.

Knobbly rudraksha nuts, subtly varied in size and shape, are juxtaposed effectively with the sophisticated smooth glass beads

Silver brass bells add an off-beat texture and as they actually ring when the wearer moves, they increase the appeal to the senses

Shiny beads blend with smooth, glossy with hammered and embossed.

Tiny blue rocailles help the necklace to hang smoothly and, echoed at the clasp, give this Indian-inspired piece of jewellery a flowing grace

This shape, which echoes the central bead, is made up from three beads

Flashes of colour, in the form of Venetian millefiori and fused two-coloured beads, throw the metal into relief.

MAKING THE MOST OF A SHAPE

The dominant shape in this necklace, exemplified in the central lozenge-shaped millefiori bead, is echoed around the necklace. The pattern is broken up by sections of silver beads.

CREATING DIFFERENT SHAPES

The same beads can be threaded together in varying orders or combined with other beads to create a different-shaped effect to the eye. Both the shapes shown here would look good suspended from an earring fitting as well as threaded onto hat or lapel pins.

When combined with flat disc-shaped beads, this large metal bead becomes lozenge-like in shape, as used to great effect in the necklace above.

When combined with silver spheres, the same bead looks altogether more rounded and bulbous.

Size and weight

The size and weight of beads you use in a necklace determine the way it hangs and how easy it is to wear, as well as its appearance. Small, light beads produce jewellery that is delicate and light enough to wear everyday. Large, heavier beads can create a more substantial necklace with a pronounced hang, which might be more suitable for evenings and special occasions. When choosing beads, remember that a small bead is not necessarily light, nor a large bead heavy, and that the distribution of weight within a necklace affects the way in which the beads hang.

Although large, these metal beads are very light, so you can use quite a lot without making the necklace too heavy.

Separated by a simple silver disc, each bead lies happily in its position and its shape can be clearly seen.

Rocailles look effective when blended with one large bead.

PENDANT
Weight determines the lie of a necklace, thus a large central bead or pendant will give the necklace a V-shaped appearance.

MIXING SIZE AND WEIGHT
A wealth of materials and weights, these beads do not swamp each other and each one stands out individually. The eye is struck by the chunky glass tubes at the centre and passes up to the heavy black spheres.

USING LARGE BEADS
With the introduction of large, important-looking beads throughout, a piece of jewellery makes a statement.

CHOOSING A THREAD

Before starting to string a necklace you must choose a thread to suit your beads. Using the wrong thread might result in a necklace which hangs strangely, kinks or even breaks. When estimating how much thread you need, always add half as much again for attaching fasteners and tying knots.

Silk thread is best for semi-precious beads and other beads with finely-drilled holes.

Nylon thread is used with light plastic, ceramic, wood and glass beads.

Nylon monofilament is ideal for heavier beads, but is not suitable for metal beads.

Tiger tail is the best thread for heavy beads and sharp beads.

By using beads which are similar in size and shape, you can create a necklace which hangs in a circular way.

The facets add a new shape to the necklace and catch the light to brighten the dense black.

The large beads separate and show off the four-strand sections of matching medium-sized Picasso beads.

USING SIMILAR SIZED BEADS

This necklace uses beads which are all of a similar shape and size, running in an easy-to-follow pattern. This gives the piece an easy fluidity and simplicity.

RANDOM WEIGHTS

Made up of many strands of black rocailles, this necklace is light to wear. To help it hang well, extra weight is provided by heavier faceted beads spaced randomly throughout the front section.

SIDE WEIGHTS

Weighted equally at the sides and in the middle with large metal beads, this multi-strand necklace hangs slightly to the sides, making a D shape.

Reds

At the fiery end of the colour spectrum, flaming red beads fused with burning orange create jewellery full of warmth and extravagance. Red beads range from Chinese cinnabar to scarlet and crimson glass. Orange is produced in shades of earthy terracotta and stinging salmon. Pile up beads in different shades of red in multi-stranded necklaces, and for relief add a flash of silver or purest white.

The heat of red and orange beads can be cooled by adding a shade from the other end of the colour spectrum, here discs of turquoise.

Blues

With their rich jewel-like colours, blue beads are the royalty of the bead world, long revered for their magical powers and worn by the most important members of society. Here in a feast of summer fruit, beads in blackberry and blueberry shades look good enough to eat when spiced with raspberry and rich plum-coloured beads in a necklace or earrings. Whether made from glass, ceramic or pearlized plastic, blue beads blended with a hint of silver shine against a paisley shawl for day, and add brilliance to grosgrain or shot taffeta by night. To temper the vibrancy, introduce iris and lilac.

Different materials in varying shades of blue and purple combine successfully in a necklace and matching earrings. Stunning Venetian glass beads, some dual-coloured in burgundy and azure, some with goldstone decoration, are mixed with claret-stained wood, pearlized mauve plastic and textured silver.

Pastels

In pale shades of pink, peach, apricot and lilac, pastel-coloured beads lend themselves to romantic, old-fashioned jewellery such as ropes of pearls and simple floral pendants. Choose plum-tinted leaf beads and frosted flower shapes with a blush of pink, and combine them with satin-finished pearly discs: perfect to wear with sheer silk chiffon or white cotton organdie. Blend sugar-almond shades of blue, pink and pale yellow with the occasional darker bead in long ropes to loop over a dusty pink shawl.

A mix of pale pastels in powder blue, faded rose and mint delicately merge when strung together in bead jewellery.

Black & grey

Strong, stark and simple, black beads strung together create jewellery with a purity of line that makes a sweeping statement when worn with a plain black dress or tuxedo. Highlight black with a forge of metals: silver, pewter and brass, riveted with raw edges or smoothly polished. For a more controlled look, combine charcoal-coloured glass and jet beads with the soft smoky shades of sepia horn and eggshell plastic.

A harmony of old and new is demonstrated in the careful teaming of costly antique beads, such as this silver filigree, with easily-available contemporary fashion beads in shiny ceramic.

Greens

Fresh and clean, these watery colours are reminiscent of sparkling light dancing on the waves. Used together in necklaces, bracelets and earrings, they create a cool, summery effect, the perfect counterpart to the palest of crushed silks or stiffly-starched creamy linen. Experiment with beads of different materials and hues, mixing chunks of rich turquoise with pale greens and plastic aquamarine beads with moss-tinted wood. For a contrasting effect, add a dappling of sunshine yellow.

To the basic palette of olive, turquoise and leaf green, add sparkle and highlights with shiny silver beads, and a dash of yellow or purest blue.

Neutrals

Subtle, delicate shades of sand, stone and cream, illuminated with rich gold, are the hues that offset the skin's natural glow. Beads in these colours are often products of the natural world: horn and bone, agate, pearl and exotic shells. For the smoothest of looks, blend cream-coloured jewellery with long languid crêpe and softly wrapped jersey in tones of butter, apricot and toffee.

Tiny rocailles and larger pearl beads adorn the lacy edging of coffee-coloured silk trousers, illuminating the delicately faded colour.

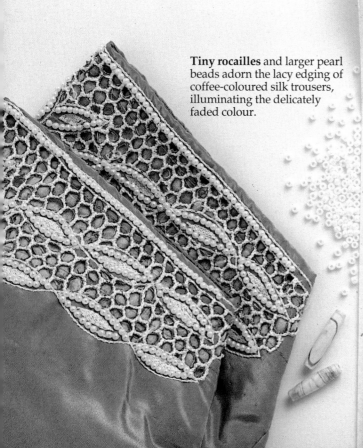

Browns

Organic or modern-looking, brown beads can be hewn from nature or produced in plastic. Woods of all types, horn, seeds and husks, with their irregular shapes and mottled colours, are rich and warm to wear. Punctuate strings of deep chestnut and mahogany-coloured beads with a touch of gold in the form of embossed brass beads. Add fake tortoiseshell or richly-lacquered beads to enhance the vitality with highlights of honey.

Antique Himalayan beads made from petrified wood embody the earthy appeal of brown beads. Varying in colour from deep chocolate to russet, they give an exotic, warm feel to jewellery. Inexpensive brass beads lift and lighten the heavier note of the browns.

Yellows

Warm, spicy yellow and amber beads blend together to form jewellery that is rich, bold and full of vitality. Naturally-coloured horn, coral and amber beads are each made up of hues ranging from pale apricot to terracotta. Yellow beads, usually man-made and dyed, include marigold-stained wood and sharp citrus-coloured ceramics. Agate and meerschaum temper the vibrancy with a touch of cream, while matt gold beads add sophistication.

Close in the colour spectrum, orange and yellow mix together easily. This bold, stylish choker, threaded on a buttercup-yellow lace, combines heavy orange glass beads and simple tangerine-tinted wood with lemon-coloured ovals and gold rings.

Themes
& special
occasions

Featuring inspiring jewellery for many
occasions and seasons, influenced by cultures
with ancient bead traditions, this section will
help you build up your own designs. Be
stimulated by the subtle magic of Indian
necklaces or the festive colours of
Christmas earrings, then follow the
practical steps to make selected pieces
of jewellery. Using the ideas as a basis
for your needs, you can adapt the
jewellery to suit an outfit, an event
or your own style.

Evening wear

A special evening occasion is the ideal time to dress up in dramatic jewellery and opulent beaded accessories. Combine the most sophisticated black faceted glass beads with a sprinkling of glittering gold beads to create dazzling necklaces and matching pins, drop earrings and bracelets. Swirls of tiny rocailles and bugles are easily sewn onto a bag, scarf or wrap, gloves and hat, and ornate fringing or rich tassels complete the picture.

A dramatic velvet hat is adorned with gold beads, rocailles and bugles, those in the centre forming a tassel. When beading thicker fabrics, use strong polyester thread in a colour to match the beads or the fabric.

An ornate pin for a lapel or hat is made by either gluing a few beads in place, or securing with a French crimp. A matt gold bead tones well with the sparkling rondelles.

Drop earrings echo the black and gold theme. The large black beads have been brushed with gold paint before threading.

An evening bag, edged with gold bugles, is beaded (see pages 120 - 1) before the lining is added. Backing thin fabric with a heavier material and sewing through both helps retain the shape.

Gloves are easily beaded. If the fabric needs to be washable, use glass, ceramic and plastic beads, not natural stones.

A stunning choker and matching cluster bracelet (right) combine gold rosebud beads with black glass. Both are made by the pinning method (see page 117).

A velvet wrap, decorated with embroidered whirls and a beaded fringe, provides an eyecatching complement to the bag and hat.

A multi-strand necklace (right) of gold and black rocailles is simply twisted (see page 80).

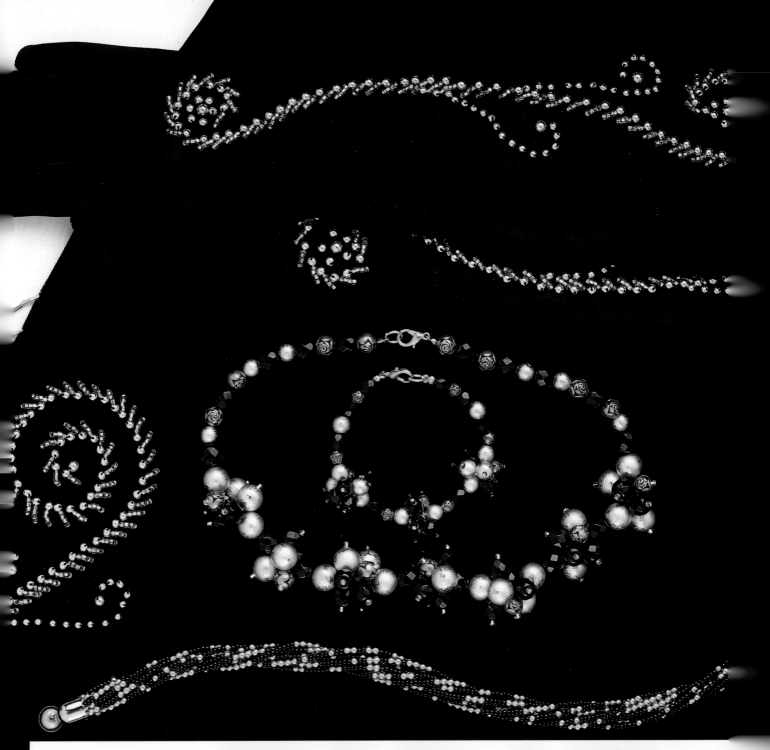

BEADING A WRAP

Plan your design on graph paper and transfer it with tailor's chalk to the fabric before attaching the beads. Alternatively, tack a tissue paper template to your work, pulling it off as you complete each section. Use a fine needle and a double thickness of thread. Secure the first and last beads by oversewing on the reverse side of the fabric.

1 Work the fabric from back to front, bringing the needle up through the bead and down immediately beside it. Bring the needle up a bead's width away.

2 Work on the outer side of the first row of beads. Thread on 4 rocailles and secure at an angle. At the curve take the needle across the back of the fabric.

3 Continue sewing rocailles on the outer side of the central row of beads until the scroll is complete. Finish the final swirl of beads, working as in step 1.

Evening wear

An evening bracelet of faceted glass is finished with gimp to protect the thread from fraying against the clasp.

FINISHING A BRACELET WITH GIMP

Ingredients *black facet*: 2 x 7 mm, 20 x 10 mm; *gold facet*: 8 x 7 mm, 6 x 10 mm; *gold bicone*: 4 small, 1 large; *gold swirl*: 14 x 4 mm. Large three row clasp, 2 m nylon thread, 6 pieces 5 mm gimp, 2 gold spacer bars.

1 Tie a slip knot in double thread twice the bracelet length (top). Attach a wire needle. Pick up one bead, gimp and a clasp loop. Pass back through the bead (above).

2 Pull the gimp gently through the loop to position it, then thread on the beads, as shown. Pass through the outer hole of the spacer bar after the 5th bead.

3 At the end thread through more gimp and the last bead again (top). Cut off the needle and knot over the main thread. Unslip the first knot and do the same (above).

Rocaille rope to twist around the neck.

Tassel earrings (see page 115) made with the same beads as the twisted rope.

MAKING A LONG ROPE

Ingredients *gold bead*: about 700 x 3 mm; *rocaille*: about 1,600 opaque black. 7 m nylon thread, 2 bell caps, 1 screw fastener clasp, 2 headpins.

1 Thread 8 strands, leaving 15 cm spare thread. String gold and black beads in bands of colour.

2 Knot the strands together near the beads. Bend a headpin and hook it through the knot.

3 Thread a cap over the pin so the strands sit inside. Cut off the excess pin and loop it to the clasp.

The beads used in the evening bracelet can be strung with large black balls to create a less dressy necklace.

Choker combining a variety of beads with different textures clustered together.

Cluster evening bracelet.

Long black rope, enlivened with gold filigree beads.

MAKING A CLUSTER NECKLACE

Ingredients *gold swirl*: 6 x 8 mm, 22 x 12 mm; *rosebud*: 15 x 10 mm; *black facet*: 47 x 10 mm; *rocaille*: 52 silver-lined transparent. 2 calotte crimps, 52 short headpins, 1 m fishing line, 1 clip, 1 jump ring.

1 Using the pinning method (see page 117) thread up all 52 pins before threading. Make 14 x 12 mm swirl, 31 x 10 mm facet and 7 rosebud pins: start each with a rocaille stopper.

2 Squeeze on a calotte (see page 116) and thread these beads to make the run-in: rosebud, facet, rosebud, facet, 6 mm swirl, facet, 6 mm swirl, rosebud, facet, rosebud, 6mm swirl, facet.

3 Thread on a 12 mm swirl, then randomly string up 7 pins to make the first side cluster. Finish the cluster with a 12 mm swirl.

4 Add facet, 7 pins, facet. Make 3 clusters of 8 pins: start and end clusters 1 and 3 with a swirl, 2 with a facet. Repeat the side clusters and run-in. Finish with a calotte. Attach the clasp.

MAKING CLUSTER EARRINGS

Cluster earrings match the choker and bracelet.

Ingredients *black facet*: 20 x 10 mm; *gold swirl*: 2 x 4 mm, 8 x 12 mm; *rosebud*: 8 x 10 mm; *black rocaille*: 36. 37 headpins, 2 clips with a loop.

1 Using the same technique as above, make 36 pins: 20 facet, 8 x 12 mm swirl, 8 rosebud. Hook 9 pins onto a looped headpin.

2 Thread on a 4 mm swirl, then the other 9 pins. Loop the top of the pin and hang from a fitting.

Summer garden

Pretty and fresh, this jewellery in pinks, lilac and lavender is ideal for tea parties, picnics and lazing in the sunshine. The perfect beads to string in summer jewellery are delicate plastic flowers and leaves, hand-blown sparkling glass which catches the light, and lustrous pearlized shapes in pastel shades.

Blown glass beads dominate this fragile-looking necklace. Each hollow bead is strung onto a headpin and looped into the next (see page 117).

Made wholly of glass beads, this necklace features crumb, trail and marbled lampwork effects.

A romantic rope combines opaline rocailles with oval blown glass beads. The three strands threaded with rocailles pass through the centre of the hollow beads.

A matching necklace and earrings mix decal ceramic beads with liquid silver.

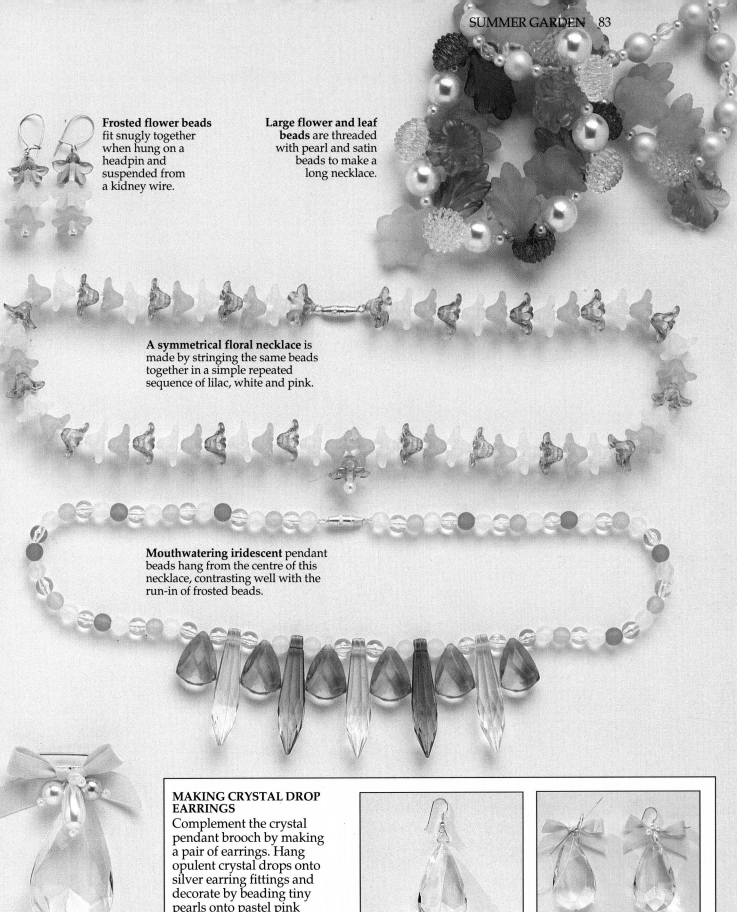

Frosted flower beads fit snugly together when hung on a headpin and suspended from a kidney wire.

Large flower and leaf beads are threaded with pearl and satin beads to make a long necklace.

A symmetrical floral necklace is made by stringing the same beads together in a simple repeated sequence of lilac, white and pink.

Mouthwatering iridescent pendant beads hang from the centre of this necklace, contrasting well with the run-in of frosted beads.

Suspend a large crystal drop from a pin-back brooch and decorate with a bow and pearls.

MAKING CRYSTAL DROP EARRINGS

Complement the crystal pendant brooch by making a pair of earrings. Hang opulent crystal drops onto silver earring fittings and decorate by beading tiny pearls onto pastel pink ribbon tied in a bow.

1 Squeeze a triangle into the drop, slipping in the fitting loop too. Sew a few beads on the front of a bow (see page 118).

2 Sew the bow to the back of the triangle with a new thread, securing each stitch by sewing around the loop on the fitting.

Festive jewellery

Wear jewellery in rich red, green and gold, mixed with a touch of black to add depth, to herald the festive season. Extravagant beaded jewellery designs capture the party mood, such as golden hoops hung with bells or ornate necklaces incorporating shiny balls and clusters of pendants. To present your Christmas gifts decorate boxes with beaded designs.

Shiny and matt beads work well together in a heavy necklace strung on tiger tail.

Ornate hoops hung with filigree beads and bells (see page 87) swing and jingle as you move.

Hand-painted beads descend in symmetrical pairs separated by rough glass and brass beads.

Unvarnished hand-painted beads look good strung as a simple rope.

PAINTING WOOD BEADS

Use gouache paint to decorate unvarnished wood beads, and to vary the effect add coats of different colours. Before starting to paint, design the pattern on paper.

1 Shave the end of a barbecue stick and spear a bead. Paint the base colour and let it dry.

2 Add the second colour, leave it to dry then paint the third coat and so on. Varnish for a glossy effect.

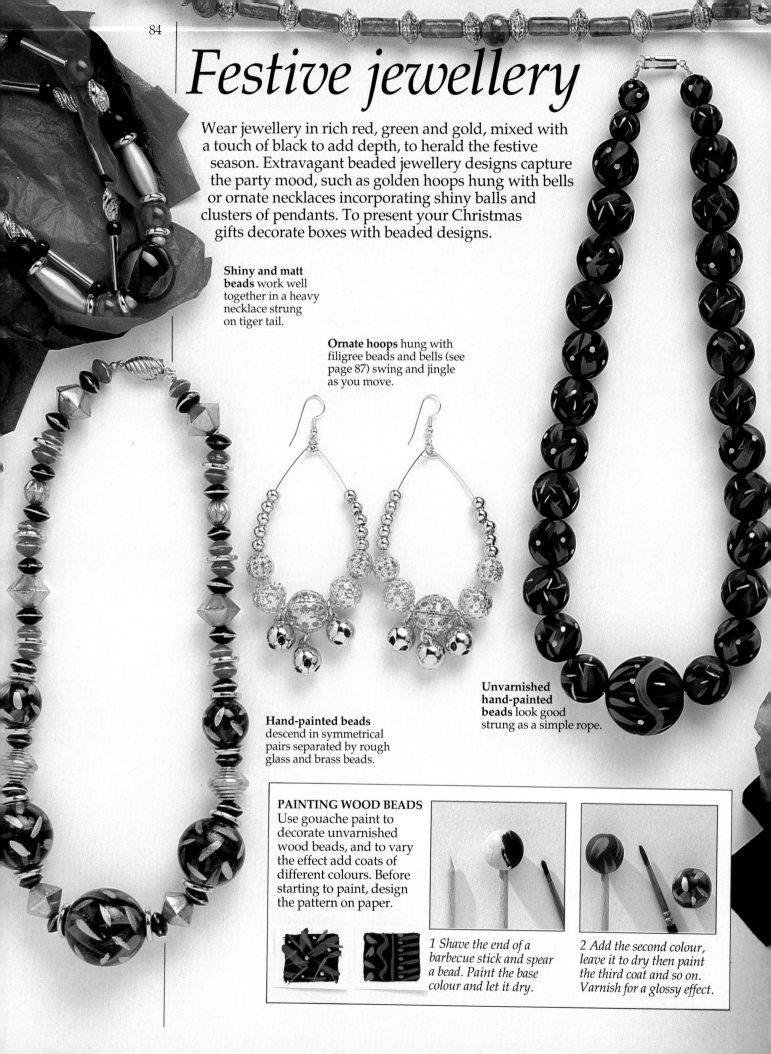

Scarlet spheres and tubes, each separated by a gold disc, form this long necklace.

A matching necklace and bracelet combine black wooden shapes with bright red ceramics and glossy plastic beads in metallic colours.

Tartan ribbon sewn with beads (see page 118) makes a delightful Christmas brooch.

String up lengths of silver-lined rocailles and bugles on nylon thread to swathe the branches of your Christmas tree.

Bulbous matt gold beads with a burnished appearance are simply strung together to make a long rope.

Decorate a gift box by covering a cardboard box with fabric, and beading (see pages 120 - 1) a delicate design in festive-coloured rocailles.

Golden beads are strung onto headpins and looped to gilt earhooks.

Festive jewellery

A necklace of malachite beads, with their ivy leaf colour, is ideal to wear on Christmas Day.

MAKING A PENDANT NECKLACE

Ingredients *bell*: 12 black, 4 small tan; *daisy*: 6 red frosted, 8 green clear; *heart*: 7 red; *leaf*: 1 small green frosted; *pearl*: 12 green 6 mm, 1 large tan drop; *wood*: 12 red 6 mm; *plastic*: 12 tan frosted 6 mm; *rocaille*: 70 black. 1 torpedo clasp, 24 gilt headpins, 1 m nylon thread.

Festive pendants are threaded onto this necklace between the beads.

1 Pin the hearts and bells (see page 117). Pin a drop: rocaille, tan pearl, black bell, heart, leaf, black bell.

2 Knot onto the clasp, finish off the tail (see page 116) and thread 6 times: 3 rocailles, 6 mm tan, 6 mm red, 6 mm pearl.

3 Thread: heart, black bell, green daisy, 3 rocailles, black and tan bell, red daisy, 3 rocailles. Repeat. Heart, black bell, green daisy, 8 rocailles, red daisy, pinned drop.

4 Repeat steps 2 and 3 in reverse, then tie onto the other loop on the clasp. Thread back and knot over the main thread (see page 116). Cut off the extra thread.

MAKING A PAIR OF HANGING EARRINGS

Ingredients *pearl*: 2 large drops; *heart*: 4 red; *bell*: 4 black; *leaf*: 4 small green; *daisy*: 2 red frosted, 2 green clear; *rocaille*: 16 black. 12 gilt headpins, 2 gilt kidney wires.

Hanging earrings complement the necklace.

1 Pin the hearts and bells (see page 117). Thread on a pin: rocaille, pearl, rocaille, heart, black bell, leaf, black bell, heart, leaf, rocaille. Form a loose loop. Make a loop on a pin and thread: 2 rocailles, red daisy, 1 rocaille, green daisy, 2 rocailles.

2 Make a loop in the top of the second pin and suspend it from the loop on the kidney wire. Slip the loop on the first pin into the eye of the second and close by squeezing it with flat-nosed pliers.

Carnelian beads in deepest red are spaced out with small gold filler beads.

Matt gold bead earrings match the bulbous rope on page 85.

Link annular beads together with jump rings to create a simple bracelet.

MAKING A WOODEN BRACELET

Ingredients *ring-shaped wood bead: 4 red, 4 black, 3 green. 23 jump rings, 1 clip fastener.*

1 Attach a jump ring to each wooden bead, by opening the ring sideways with flat-nosed pliers. Fix a ring to the loop on the clasp, leaving it slightly open, to link into the first black bead.

2 Attach a second jump ring to the other side of each bead, slipping in the jump ring on the previous bead before you close it.

Lengths of rocailles are threaded down through a filigree bead and back up on the other side.

Mix gold bells with filigree beads to create a pair of special Christmas earrings.

MAKING BELL EARRINGS

Ingredients *gilt filigree: 4 x 10 mm, 4 x 12 mm, 2 x 15 mm; gilt bell: 6 x 10 mm; gilt bead: 20 x 4 mm. 2 x 15 cm lengths of brass wire, 2 x 5mm, 6 x 8 mm gilt jump rings, 2 gilt earhooks.*

1 Attach 4 bells to the 8 mm rings. Join the other bells to 8 mm rings and attach to the 15 mm filigree beads.

2 Thread onto each wire: 5 beads, 10 mm filigree, bell, 15 mm filigree (with the bell hanging down), bell, 12 mm and 10 mm filigrees, 5 beads. Loop all ends.

3 Thread a 5 mm ring through both loops in the end of the wire. Link through the loop on the earring fitting and squeeze with snipe-nosed pliers.

To give jewellery at Christmas, such as this necklace and matching brooch pin, wrap it in berry red and ivy green tissue paper.

A hat pin, which would look good on a crimson velvet hat, is made using the technique on page 118.

Wedding day

A wedding day is the time to wear simple, classically elegant jewellery and accessories. For the bride and her attendants matching necklaces and earrings in pearly white beads or semi-precious rose quartz are ideal, and delicate rocailles and bugles can be sewn onto the wedding dress or dot the train and veil.

Delicate floral earrings match the clematis necklace.

Clematis flower beads are threaded to hang forward on this necklace. Use cotton thread, which does not stretch like nylon thread.

Beading (see pages 120 - 1) enriches the bodice of this exquisite wedding dress.

MAKING A CLEMATIS NECKLACE

Ingredients *flower bead*: 9 clematis; *white pearl*: 50 x 4 mm, 38 x 6 mm. 1 torpedo clasp, 1 m cotton thread.

1 Knot onto the clasp and thread the run-in with 4 mm and 6 mm pearl 11 times. End with a 4 mm.

2 Thread a clematis and pick up a 4 mm pearl. To make the clematis lie flat, thread back through it.

3 Add 4 mm pearl, 2 x 6 mm pearl, 4 mm pearl, the next clematis and so on. Finish with a run-in.

KNOTTING BETWEEN BEADS

Knotting between each rose quartz bead looks attractive and protects the beads from chafing or rolling away if the necklace breaks.

Ingredients *rose quartz: 49 beads. 1 silver clasp, 1.5 m silk thread.*

1 Pass a double-threaded wire needle through a clasp. Knot around the thread. Pick up a bead.

2 Press the bead firmly against the knot. Then make a knot in the thread near it.

3 Ease the knot towards the bead with a point, such as round-nosed plier tips, then pull it tight. Repeat the process until you reach the last bead. Thread through the clasp and knot between clasp and bead.

A bridesmaid's set of matching mottled pink earrings, bracelet and necklace will be adored by any young attendant.

SEWING ON A BEADED TRIMMING

To obtain the look of an elegant edging of beads on the bottom of a hem, sleeve or train without any time-consuming bead sewing, stitch on a ready-threaded beaded trimming, available from department stores and haberdashers.

1 Tack the bead trim to the hem, then start stitching the bottom of the trim using back stitch. This anchors the whole piece.

2 Finish by stitching down the top edge, then carefully remove the large tacking stitches.

Classical elegance in pearl and diamanté earrings and choker. These would also look good in warm ivory or pale apricot beads.

Children's jewellery

Children love to make and wear jewellery. They enjoy playing with colour and from about six years old are able, first with supervision, to use a blunt needle and thread and experiment on their own. Simple threading with elastic, gluing motifs onto brooch backs and sewing brightly coloured wooden beads are the techniques that keep children happy for hours.

Simple wooden beads (above) strung on nylon thread are knotted onto a barrel clasp (see page 116).

Multi-coloured beads in primary colours can be strung in numerous ways.

A small teddy bear is suspended from the centre of this bracelet to dangle over the wrist.

Fruit motifs are threaded between wooden beads in primary colours. There are nine beads between each motif to keep the necklace symmetrical.

Plywood motifs can be glued onto brooch backs or made into pendants by squeezing a triangle through the hole (see page 114). Thread the pendant onto a necklace or an earring finding loop.

Glass alphabet beads form an interesting centrepiece and can spell out names.

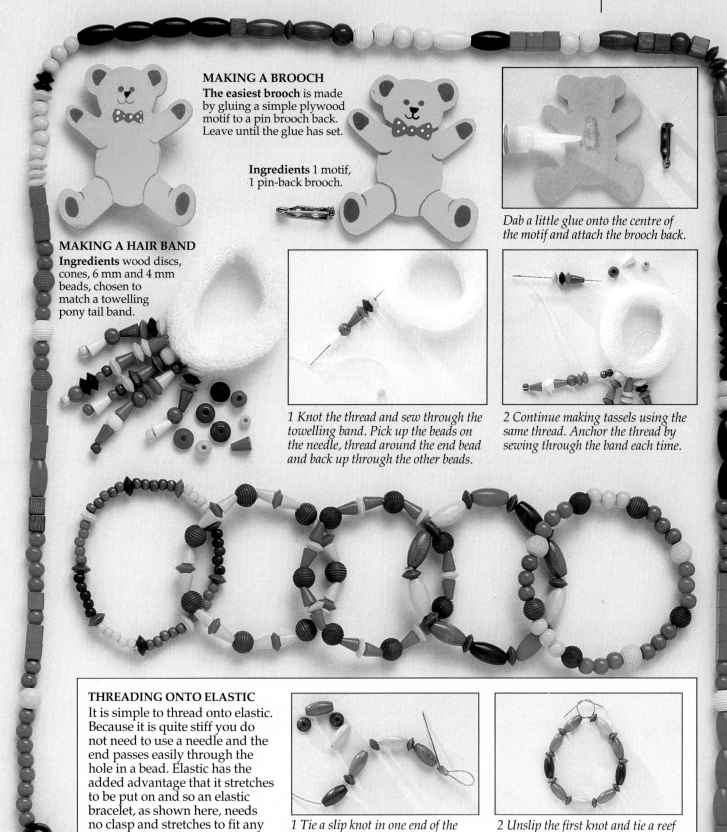

MAKING A BROOCH

The easiest brooch is made by gluing a simple plywood motif to a pin brooch back. Leave until the glue has set.

Ingredients 1 motif, 1 pin-back brooch.

Dab a little glue onto the centre of the motif and attach the brooch back.

MAKING A HAIR BAND

Ingredients wood discs, cones, 6 mm and 4 mm beads, chosen to match a towelling pony tail band.

1 Knot the thread and sew through the towelling band. Pick up the beads on the needle, thread around the end bead and back up through the other beads.

2 Continue making tassels using the same thread. Anchor the thread by sewing through the band each time.

THREADING ONTO ELASTIC

It is simple to thread onto elastic. Because it is quite stiff you do not need to use a needle and the end passes easily through the hole in a bead. Elastic has the added advantage that it stretches to be put on and so an elastic bracelet, as shown here, needs no clasp and stretches to fit any wrist size.

1 Tie a slip knot in one end of the elastic, which should be about 20 cm long. Thread beads on the other end.

2 Unslip the first knot and tie a reef knot by passing right over left and under, left over right and under.

The African look

Inspired by the colours of Africa's landscapes and deserts, this jewellery collection is based on tones of brown, terracotta and cream. The beads used are fashioned from natural materials gathered across the globe: shells and coral from the ocean; coco, palm and banana leaf from the forest.

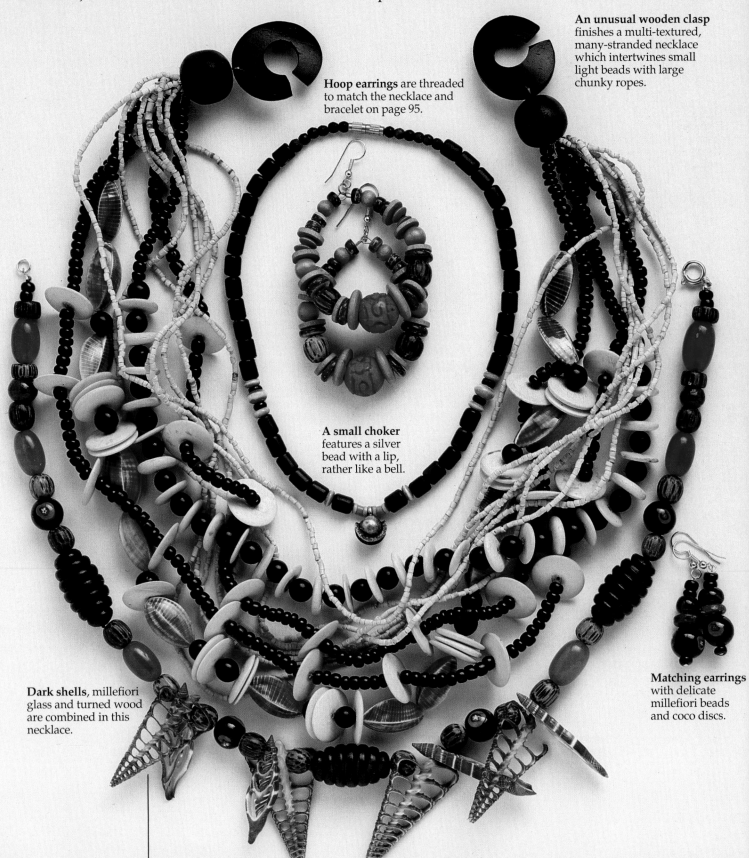

An unusual wooden clasp finishes a multi-textured, many-stranded necklace which intertwines small light beads with large chunky ropes.

Hoop earrings are threaded to match the necklace and bracelet on page 95.

A small choker features a silver bead with a lip, rather like a bell.

Dark shells, millefiori glass and turned wood are combined in this necklace.

Matching earrings with delicate millefiori beads and coco discs.

A pendant choker has each strand individually threaded onto wire and fastened with a calotte crimp. The sections are then threaded onto the main strand.

A twisted bracelet is made by threading beads onto a length of wire with a loop at one end. Shape the bracelet around a round object and finish with another loop.

Orange wood and brass earrings worn by a carved Ghanaian fertility doll.

Four shells, combined into one bead, have been threaded onto an eyepin and hung from a fitting.

A choker of flat ebony discs has light beads threaded through the hole on each disc so that the necklace will lie flat on the neck.

THREADING DISCS TO LIE FLAT

This technique can be used with any flat discs and small rocaille-sized beads. Start the necklace by making a run-in on two threads, then divide them before starting to thread on the discs.

1 On each thread string up a disc's width of beads. Weave one thread down through the hole in a disc, weave the other thread up through it and so on.

2 To add another row of beads, pass a thread 3 times the length of the necklace through the hole in the first disc with an equal amount of thread on each side.

3 Pick up enough beads to reach the hole in the next disc and weave the thread through. Repeat with the other end of the thread so the threads cross.

The African look

A long necklace mixes shiny flat beads with lozenge-shaped banana leaf beads, spaced with small coco tubes.

A short necklace of horn beads is threaded onto cord and knotted (see page 89) between each bead. A button hole clasp is fastened with a button chosen to match the beads.

Bamboo beads are used on a long brooch which fastens back on itself (see page 118).

A chunky necklace is threaded on two strands which are separated at key points (see page 117).

A three-strand necklace uses a horn spacer bar at each side to keep the threads evenly spaced. The simple shell at the centre hangs on the breast bone.

A long necklace made up of beads from all over the world.

Matching the necklace above, this bracelet uses a three row clasp.

MAKING A THREE-STRAND NECKLACE

Ingredients *coco*: 108 x 6 mm, 42 x 10 mm; *coral*: 2 x 20 mm, 4 x 12 mm, 4 x 15 mm; *wood*: 10 x 8 mm white, 7 x 10 mm plain; *tan wood*: 36 discs, 20 x 8 mm, 28 lentils, 4 big tubes; *palm*: 6 x 8 mm; *clay*: 18 beads. 4 calottes, 9 mm bolt ring, 1 jump ring, 1 m fishing line.

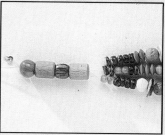

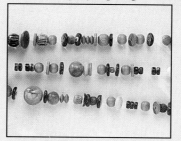

1 *Cut the line into 3, leaving 20 cm extra on each. Thread the rows randomly, placing the large beads away from the centre.*

2 *Pass all 3 rows through tube, 8 mm palm, tube, 12 mm coral on both sides. Knot the strands together and add a calotte.*

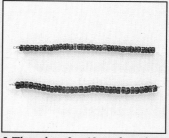

3 *Thread up 2 x 12 cm lengths of 6 mm coco beads for each side of the necklace. Start and finish each strand with a calotte crimp.*

4 *Join the calottes on the main section to the calottes on the side lengths. Put a bolt ring and jump ring on the other ends.*

MAKING A BRACELET

Ingredients *cinnabar*: 1 bead; *palm*: 2 big discs, 4 lozenges, 6 x 8 mm; *coco*: 25 x 6 mm, 10 x 10 mm; *tan wood*: 12 x 6 mm, 6 x 8 mm, 24 discs, 26 lentils, 2 tubes, 4 big rings; *white wood*: 8 x 8 mm. 6 calottes, 1 three row clasp, 1 m nylon thread.

1 *Follow step 1 above with a cinnabar bead in the centre of row 1, tan tubes in rows 2 and 3.*

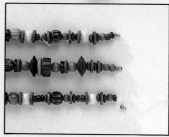

2 *Tie a knot at the ends of each row and squeeze a calotte crimp onto both ends.*

3 *Fix the 6 calottes to the 6 clasp loops. Ensure the row with the cinnabar bead is in the centre.*

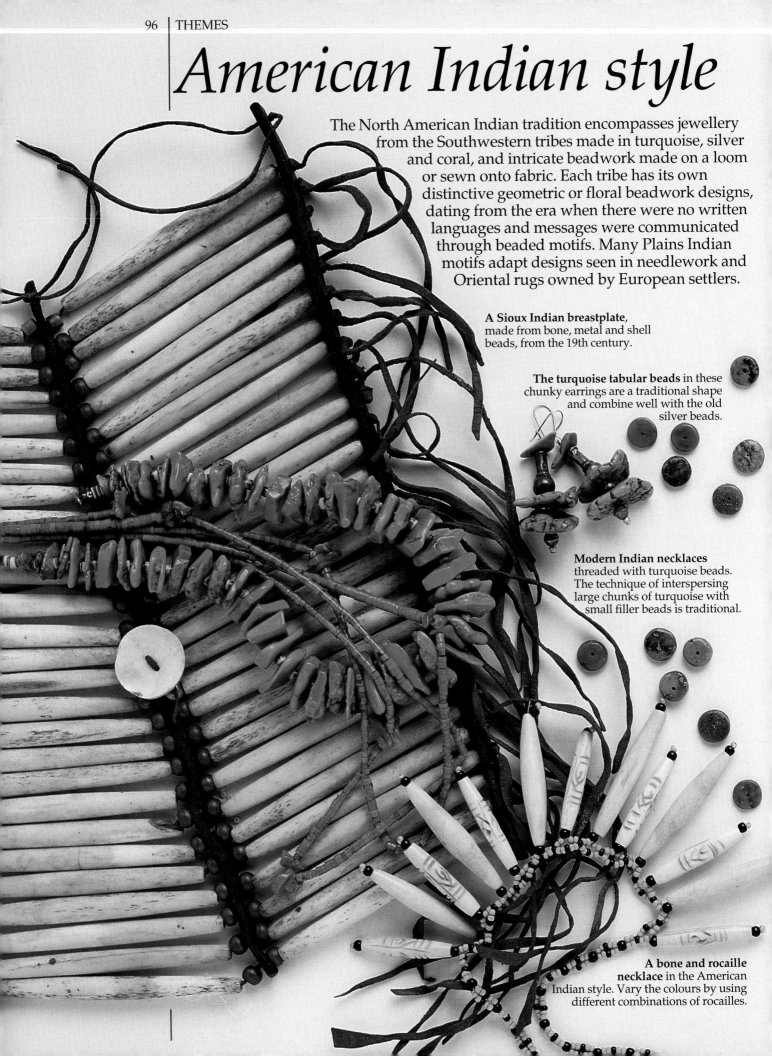

American Indian style

The North American Indian tradition encompasses jewellery from the Southwestern tribes made in turquoise, silver and coral, and intricate beadwork made on a loom or sewn onto fabric. Each tribe has its own distinctive geometric or floral beadwork designs, dating from the era when there were no written languages and messages were communicated through beaded motifs. Many Plains Indian motifs adapt designs seen in needlework and Oriental rugs owned by European settlers.

A Sioux Indian breastplate, made from bone, metal and shell beads, from the 19th century.

The turquoise tabular beads in these chunky earrings are a traditional shape and combine well with the old silver beads.

Modern Indian necklaces threaded with turquoise beads. The technique of interspersing large chunks of turquoise with small filler beads is traditional.

A bone and rocaille necklace in the American Indian style. Vary the colours by using different combinations of rocailles.

A bag is made by sewing together strips of beaded fabric. Sew a strip half the width of the others, long enough to form a handle, to both sides. To make the tassel, divide the fabric while weaving. Complete the bag by sewing all the beaded edges to chamois leather (buy two and a half times more than the size of the bag). Turn over hems in the top edges and before sewing down, line the bag with fabric stiffener and silk, and run a plastic stay through each hem.

SEWING TOGETHER STRIPS OF BEADED FABRIC

Either weave a beaded strip on a loom (see page 98) or use ready-beaded strips which you can find in craft, jewellery or antique shops. To sew the strips together you will need a thin, pliable beading needle with a small hole and double thread. To make the seam neat, use strips made from similar-sized beads and match up the pieces so that the beads butt against each other.

1 On the bottom row of the right-hand strip, thread the needle through the last 12 beads, leaving a long tail in the thread.

2 Take the needle through the first 4 beads of the row that corresponds to it on the left-hand strip and pull the needle through so the strips meet.

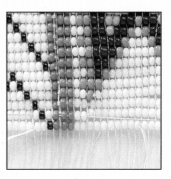

3 On the row above work from left to right. Sew through the last 4 beads on the left-hand strip, the first 4 on the right. At the end sew in both tails.

A beaded belt woven on a loom.

American Indian style

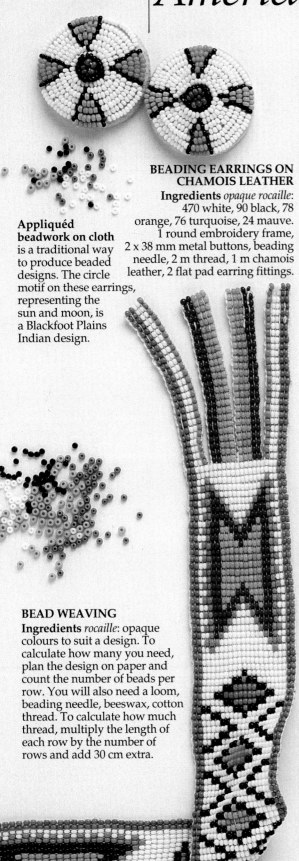

BEADING EARRINGS ON CHAMOIS LEATHER

Ingredients *opaque rocaille:* 470 white, 90 black, 78 orange, 76 turquoise, 24 mauve. 1 round embroidery frame, 2 x 38 mm metal buttons, beading needle, 2 m thread, 1 m chamois leather, 2 flat pad earring fittings.

Appliquéd beadwork on cloth is a traditional way to produce beaded designs. The circle motif on these earrings, representing the sun and moon, is a Blackfoot Plains Indian design.

1 Stretch the chamois in the frame and secure a double thread with 2 tiny stitches on the reverse. Come up at the front and thread on the first beads.

2 Coil the threaded beads. Secure another needle and double thread near the start, come up and couch (see page 120) to fit the size of the button.

3 Cut the design from the frame, 4 cm from the edge. Stretch over the teeth on the reverse of the button with large stitches. Press on the back and glue to a fitting.

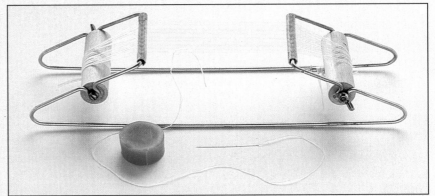

1 Thread up the loom following the manufacturer's instructions. Then thread up a beading needle with double thread and run it across the beeswax to strengthen and protect it. Knot the waxed thread around the first warp (lengthways) thread.

BEAD WEAVING

Ingredients *rocaille:* opaque colours to suit a design. To calculate how many you need, plan the design on paper and count the number of beads per row. You will also need a loom, beading needle, beeswax, cotton thread. To calculate how much thread, multiply the length of each row by the number of rows and add 30 cm extra.

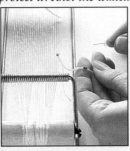

2 With the needle pick up enough beads to make one row. There is always one more warp thread than the number of beads in a row.

3 With a finger, press each bead up into the space between the warp threads. Then ease the thread they are on through without pulling it tight.

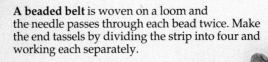

4 Pressing the beads up firmly with your finger, pass the needle back through the beads. Make sure it passes over each warp thread.

A beaded belt is woven on a loom and the needle passes through each bead twice. Make the end tassels by dividing the strip into four and working each separately.

Intricately carved beads in the shape of animals, birds and fish feature in this beautiful turquoise three-strand necklace.

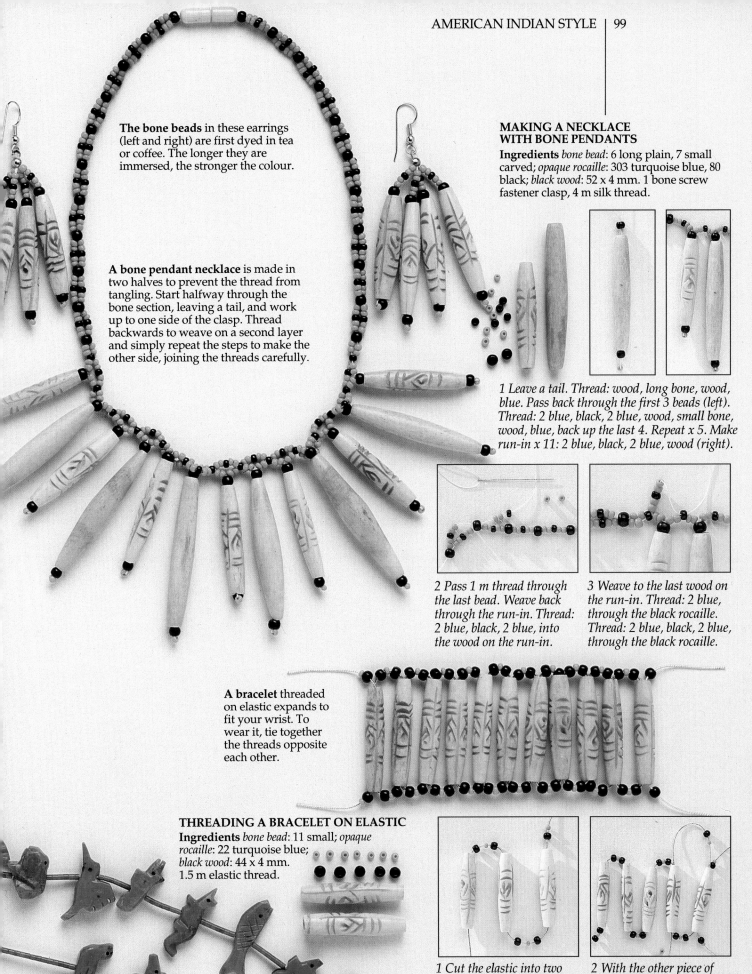

The bone beads in these earrings (left and right) are first dyed in tea or coffee. The longer they are immersed, the stronger the colour.

A bone pendant necklace is made in two halves to prevent the thread from tangling. Start halfway through the bone section, leaving a tail, and work up to one side of the clasp. Thread backwards to weave on a second layer and simply repeat the steps to make the other side, joining the threads carefully.

MAKING A NECKLACE WITH BONE PENDANTS

Ingredients *bone bead*: 6 long plain, 7 small carved; *opaque rocaille*: 303 turquoise blue, 80 black; *black wood*: 52 x 4 mm. 1 bone screw fastener clasp, 4 m silk thread.

1 *Leave a tail. Thread: wood, long bone, wood, blue. Pass back through the first 3 beads (left). Thread: 2 blue, black, 2 blue, wood, small bone, wood, blue, back up the last 4. Repeat x 5. Make run-in x 11: 2 blue, black, 2 blue, wood (right).*

2 *Pass 1 m thread through the last bead. Weave back through the run-in. Thread: 2 blue, black, 2 blue, into the wood on the run-in.*

3 *Weave to the last wood on the run-in. Thread: 2 blue, through the black rocaille. Thread: 2 blue, black, 2 blue, through the black rocaille.*

A bracelet threaded on elastic expands to fit your wrist. To wear it, tie together the threads opposite each other.

THREADING A BRACELET ON ELASTIC

Ingredients *bone bead*: 11 small; *opaque rocaille*: 22 turquoise blue; *black wood*: 44 x 4 mm. 1.5 m elastic thread.

1 *Cut the elastic into two pieces. Take one piece and thread on blue, wood, bone, wood. Repeat this sequence 11 times.*

2 *With the other piece of elastic thread blue, wood and up through the first bone, blue, wood, down through the next bone bead. Repeat.*

The Indian look

India, land of heat, spices and sandalwood, ablaze with jewel-bright fabrics, is the inspiration for elaborate, extravagant jewellery. Blend Indian silver in traditional shapes with richly coloured heavy glass beads to make opulent, boldly-designed earrings, necklaces and brooches.

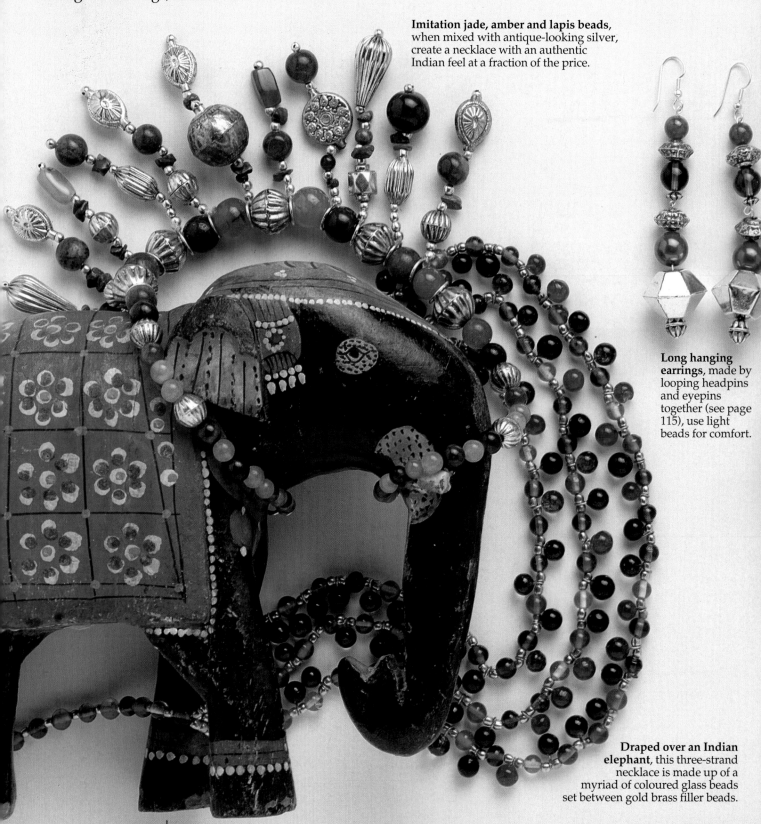

Imitation jade, amber and lapis beads, when mixed with antique-looking silver, create a necklace with an authentic Indian feel at a fraction of the price.

Long hanging earrings, made by looping headpins and eyepins together (see page 115), use light beads for comfort.

Draped over an Indian elephant, this three-strand necklace is made up of a myriad of coloured glass beads set between gold brass filler beads.

A long necklace (left) features large Indian silver beads and an adventurous colour scheme, mixing green, purple, red and blue.

Heavy necklaces threaded on tiger tail (above) use similar beads in different combinations.

Three pendants swing from a jewel-coloured brooch, giving it a fluid line.

Each bead in this delicate necklace is looped on wire (see page 117), which isolates the glorious colours.

HANGING PENDANT SECTIONS FROM A BROOCH

Brooches can be made to look more ornate by suspending beads from them. Pin up the pendant sections of beads, then with a bent headpin hang each pendant section from the bottom holes of a perforated disc brooch.

1 Thread a headpin through a perforated disc and bend it to catch the head in the hole. Cut off the excess pin.

2 Pin up the pendant pieces (see page 117). Attach to the pin on the disc by looping it.

3 Bead the front of the brooch (see page 118), then clamp on the brooch back.

The Indian look

A long rope has silver bells strung at the sides and the front, echoed with ornate goldstone-trimmed beads.

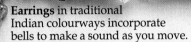

Earrings in traditional Indian colourways incorporate bells to make a sound as you move.

MAKING INDIAN-STYLE EARRINGS

Ingredients *silver brass bells*: 6 clusters; *wood*: 12 purple discs, 6 x 6 mm navy beads; *silver bead*: 12 x 6 mm; *rocaille*: 38 blue. 6 headpins, 2 earhooks.

1 Cut off the head ends of the headpins with cutters. Make a loop in the other end of the pin using round-nosed pliers, and slip in a cluster of bells.

2 Add to each pin: 2 discs, wood bead, silver bead. Then randomly thread on rocailles and a silver bead. Loop the top of each pin.

3 Slip the 3 pins into the loop on the earring finding and squeeze each loop tightly shut using snipe-nosed pliers. Repeat for the other earring.

A lapel pin is threaded (see page 118) with a two-toned indigo and plum glass bead, and topped with silver discs and balls.

Circlet earrings are attached to gold brass clips which echo the attractive brass bicone beads.

Large silver beads range round this necklace which features a deep blue glossy bead at the centre. Sherry coloured plastic pearls lighten the effect, and a hook and chain fitting ensures that you can adjust the length to suit you.

MAKING A RANDOM THREE-STRAND NECKLACE

Ingredients It is not essential to obtain the very beads used here. Rather, choose a mixture of toning colours and materials to suit your own style. Use 2 m fishing line, 2 or more calotte crimps and 1 screw fastener.

A three-strand necklace of beads in many colours and materials is caught together by a striking bead at each side.

1 Cut 3 equal lengths of thread and start threading one. Start in the middle with a large feature bead and work up each side.

2 Repeat with the other strands, making sure the thread with the feature bead is longest, the others each slightly shorter.

3 On one side pass all 3 strands through an oval bead, some flat metal discs and a large feature bead. Repeat on the other side.

4 Finish each side with calottes (see page 116) and a clasp. To make this section longer, add another short run-in on calottes.

Rejuvenating jewellery

Whether you inherit an old necklace or pick one up from a junk stall, it will often be dirty, broken and perhaps not to your taste. Old jewellery can be easily transformed: simply clean it, removing any broken or damaged beads, weak threads and ugly, tarnished clasps, then re-string either imitating the original style or using new designs to suit your wardrobe and other accessories.

TWISTED STRANDS
These beautiful beads are dirty from years of neglect, and one strand of the choker is attached to the wrong loop on the clasp.

Twisted strands are badly attached to a tarnished clasp.

DIRTY BEADS
Interesting white faceted beads from the 1930s, found cheaply at a market stall, are engrained with dirt and fitted with a cheap clasp.

A bead next to the clasp is chipped and the knot is obtrusive.

PLAIN NECKLACE
Green beads are attractive in themselves, but, when looped together with brass wire, have a rather old-fashioned feel.

Some of the loops connecting the beads are slightly open.

BADLY REPAIRED NECKLACE
This necklace seems to have been made up from a number of old necklaces. One of the strands has broken and the odd beads, including rusty metal, are arranged haphazardly.

Minor repairs, such as this knot, detract from the French glass beads.

To transform a necklace, first remove all the findings, broken beads and threads, then clean the dirty beads (see page 107). To remake, choose a suitable thread which fits the hole: a thin thread does not allow a bead to lie properly. Improvise by adding extra beads instead of re-knotting, try using contrasting beads to give extra length or a new colour scheme, turn a rope into a double length choker or leave enough beads over to make a pair of matching earrings.

Combine two necklaces in understated colours (here, the black and green) and mix in an assortment of special beads collected over the years to create a randomly-strung, long necklace with a contemporary feel.

Marry modern beads in contrasting colours with cleaned antique beads to enliven the simple white necklace.

Remake a necklace in the original style, adding a new, interesting clasp and gold filigree caps. Before breaking the necklace, study carefully the method by which it was made and draw a diagram to help you reconstruct it.

Rejuvenating jewellery

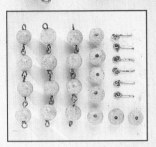

Transform the green necklace into pendant earrings looped onto a perforated disc fitting.

MAKING PENDANT EARRINGS

Ingredients *old beads:* 38 from green necklace. 20 gilt headpins, 2 perforated disc fittings.

A multi-strand necklace of old glossy French glass beads is highlighted with new gold filigree.

1 For each earring cut 3 chains of 4 beads from the old necklace and 7 single beads from their loops.

2 Cut off the head and make a loop in a pin. Add a bead and thread through the disc. Cut off the extra pin and roll over until tight. Repeat with all the single beads.

3 Fix the 3 chains to the central holes on the disc by threading a pin through the top loop of the chain. Secure as in step 2. Clamp on the disc back.

MAKING A MULTI-STRAND NECKLACE

Ingredients *old beads:* 377 French glass; *new beads:* 2 large black facets. 2 gilt filigree caps, 2 gilt headpins, 1 gilt snap fastener clasp, 3.5 m nylon thread.

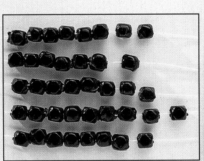

1 Cut 5 strands of 50 cm thread and leaving 10 cm spare at both ends thread 63 French glass beads on each. Knot the strands together at each end.

Matching tassel earrings hang below the jaw line.

2 Cut off the extra thread and push a bent headpin through the knot. Thread on a filigree cap and make a loop in the headpin. Repeat with the other knot.

3 Knot 50 cm thread to the loop. Thread on a glass bead, pass the tail through (see page 80). Pick up 31 beads and knot onto the clasp. Repeat on the other side.

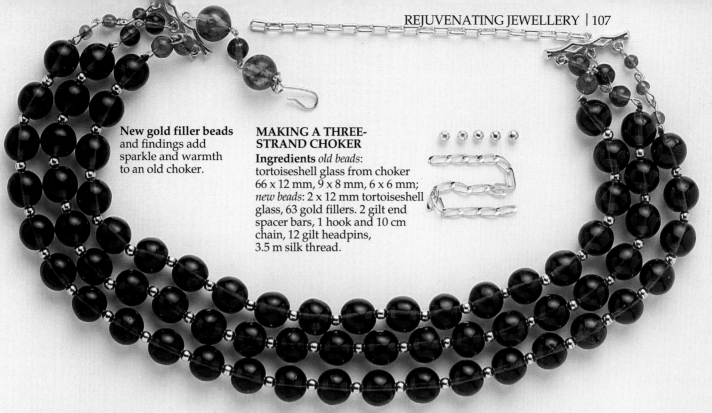

New gold filler beads and findings add sparkle and warmth to an old choker.

MAKING A THREE-STRAND CHOKER

Ingredients *old beads*: tortoiseshell glass from choker 66 x 12 mm, 9 x 8 mm, 6 x 6 mm; *new beads*: 2 x 12 mm tortoiseshell glass, 63 gold fillers. 2 gilt end spacer bars, 1 hook and 10 cm chain, 12 gilt headpins, 3.5 m silk thread.

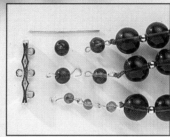

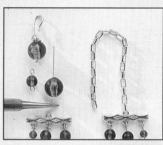

1 Pin up 9 x 8 mm beads and 6 x 6 mm beads (see page 117) and with a twisted copper needle knot the silk onto a pinned 8 mm bead. Thread on a 12 mm bead.

2 Pass the tail through the bead and knot. Thread 20 x 12 mm beads, a filler between each. Knot to a pinned 8 mm bead. Make a 22 and 24 bead strand. Knot the 24 strand to pinned 6 mm beads.

3 Join 2 pinned 6 mm beads to each end of the 24 bead strand, a pinned 8 mm bead to each end of the other strands. Join the end loops to 2 spacer bars. The 24 bead strand is on the outside.

4 Pin up 2 new 12 mm beads. Fix one to the loop on the hook, one to the spacer bar. Join them with a pinned 8 mm bead. Link the last chain loop to the other spacer bar.

THREADING A SINGLE STRAND NECKLACE

Ingredients *old beads*: 27 white facets; *new beads*: 6 x 6 mm apple coral, 40 silver flat discs, 6 small silver bicones. 1 silver clip fastener clasp, 1 split ring, 1 m nylon line.

There are enough beads in the old necklace to make a bracelet using the same method.

Angular white beads are strung with new coral and silver beads.

1 Make a knot and add a calotte (see page 116). Thread x 8 disc, facet, disc; coral, disc, facet, disc, bicone, disc, facet, disc 3 times. The last bead is the largest.

2 From the centre thread the sequence in reverse. Knot the thread and add a calotte. Squeeze the clasp loop into one calotte, a split ring into the other.

CLEANING BEADS

Clean beads in warm soapy water, lifting off built-up grime with a soft toothbrush, cotton-wool bud or chamois leather. Rinse in clean, tepid water and dry with a cloth, not abrasive tissues. Do not use solvents or immerse porous stones (pearls, coral, turquoise), delicate decoration or papier-mâché.

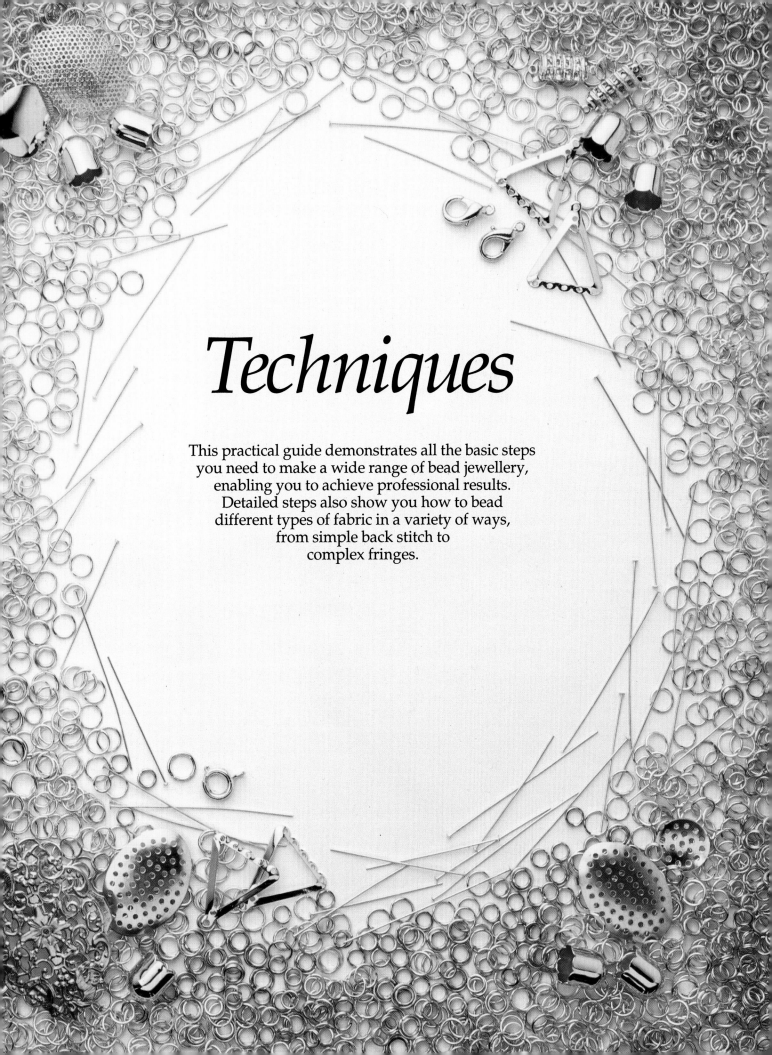

Techniques

This practical guide demonstrates all the basic steps
you need to make a wide range of bead jewellery,
enabling you to achieve professional results.
Detailed steps also show you how to bead
different types of fabric in a variety of ways,
from simple back stitch to
complex fringes.

Findings

Findings are the metal fittings used for making up jewellery. From clasps and earring wires to headpins and crimps, these are the essential pieces that transform a pile of beads into a pair of earrings or a beautiful lapel pin. Usually made in base metal and either plated with or dipped in a silver, gold or nickel solution, fittings are also made in gold and sterling silver.

NECKLACE AND BRACELET CLASPS

Clasps are the findings that attach to the ends of bracelets, necklaces, chokers and pendants. Choose which type of clasp to use by the look of the piece of jewellery.

Screw fasteners consist of two halves that screw together. The thread is attached to the loops on either side of the clasp.

Silver-plated torpedo

Gilt torpedo

Snap fasteners have two sections that hook or snap together. One end of the thread attaches to each side of the fastener.

Silver-plated shell clasp

Shell clasp in gilt

Floral clasp

Ribbed clasp

Domed gold clasp

A three row clasp has three loops to attach to necklaces and bracelets with three strands.

Pearl and silver clasp

Pearl diamanté clasp

Diamanté three row clasp

Ring clasp: ideal for a short choker.

Crystal clasp

Ring fasteners clip onto a jump ring or split ring (see page 111) at the other end of the necklace. The thread is attached to the loop on the fastener.

Interlocking fasteners   *Clips*

Bolt rings

The other half of the fastener snaps into this part of the clasp

End spacers enable you to use a one row clasp when working with three rows of beads

A hook and chain can be attached with wire to the end of a short necklace or choker to fasten it.

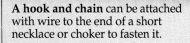

Spacer bars help keep the threads on a multi-strand necklace at a good distance from each other.

Gilt three row spacer

Silver end spacer

Gilt end spacer

Rings Attached to the end of a necklace, rings clip to ring fasteners.

Jump rings, also used for earrings.

Split rings have an overlapping wire.

Jump rings are oval or round.

Jump rings *and all loops must be opened sideways to stop the metal weakening.*

Jump ring with a ring fastener

Tags are used with bolt rings or small clips to fasten a necklace.

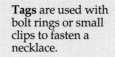

Triangles squeeze into the hole in a bead to suspend it from an earring finding or necklace.

CRIMPS

Crimps are most often used to secure the thread at the ends of a necklace. Both clasps and rings or tags attach to them.

Calotte crimps, hinged cups with a loop attached, finish off necklaces with heavier beads and thread.

Lace end crimps squeeze tightly over cotton lace or leather cords at the end of a necklace.

French crimps are tiny rings which are squeezed onto nylon and silk thread and fishing line.

The clasp is attached to the loop on the crimp

CUPS AND CAPS

Cups and caps decoratively disguise the threads at the end of a multi-strand necklace or earrings.

Cups can be threaded on either side of a bead to add decoration to necklaces.

Bead cups

Decorated bead cup

Mini bead cups

Caps are attached to the fastening and attractively hide multiple threads.

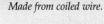

Cord caps sit over a bunch of cords.

Bell caps

Oval scalloped caps

Gimp is a fine coil which passes through the loops on a metal clasp to protect the thread from fraying.

Made from coiled wire.

BROOCH AND PIN FITTINGS

Findings for brooches and pins are easily beaded by sewing or gluing beads onto them.

Perforated disc brooch Beads are threaded through the holes with a needle and thread or on thin wire.

The back clips onto the claws on the perforated disc once the design is complete.

Pin-back brooch A large motif can be glued onto this finding or beads can be threaded through the holes with thread or on wire.

A ring with a perforated disc is beaded in the same way as a perforated disc brooch.

A hair clip is the basis for a hair accessory. Sew beads through the holes in the top.

Hat and lapel pins, in a range of sizes, are threaded with beads. Secure these with a crimp or glue.

Findings

EARRING FINDINGS

The design of earring findings has changed very little over the centuries. Fish hooks from Ancient Egypt can be seen in the British Museum.

Findings for pierced ears
A variety of fittings are made for pierced ears.

Surgical steel ear fittings do not cause allergic reactions.

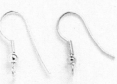

A butterfly or clutch anchors the back of an earstud.

Earhooks or fish hooks have loops from which beads are suspended.

Kidney wires are rounded and the back clips into the front.

Earstud with loop has a small ball which fits in front of the lobe.

Earstuds with cup and prong for gluing on beads with half-drilled holes.

Flat pad studs for gluing on cabochons and other beads with flat backs.

Cabochon beads

Clips and screw fittings
Use these findings for non-pierced ears and heavy earrings.

Clip with large pad and loop. — *Smaller gilt clip.* — *Delicate clips for more elegant designs.*

Large screw fitting with loop for hanging beads.

Screw ear fitting with cup and prong. Glue a half-drilled bead onto the prong.

Clips with perforated discs for threading beads onto. — *Clip with a loop.* — *Flat pad clip.* — *Rubber pieces glue to the back of the clip to prevent it from pinching the lobe.*

HEADPINS AND EYEPINS

These lengths of wire are used to make pendant earrings or necklaces. Headpins can be made into eyepins: buy them in the proportion of three to every one eyepin.

Headpins and eyepins loop arrangements together. The beads are threaded onto the pins and loops are formed in the end. These loops are then joined together.

Headpins, so called because they have a head at one end.

Eyepins have a small loop, or 'eye', at the end.

Beads are threaded onto a long eyepin and a loop, or eye, is made at the other end. Both eyes are then joined to the loop on the earring fitting.

Headpin earring — *Eyepin earring*

Equipment

Using the right equipment gives a professional finish, so invest in a good set of pliers and a wide range of threads before you start to make your own jewellery.

THREADS
The size and weight of the beads used dictates the type of thread you need.

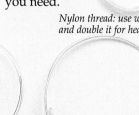

Nylon thread: use with a needle, and double it for heavy beads.

Nylon monofilament, or fishing line, for heavy beads. Knots made with this thread may slip and it becomes brittle if used with metal beads.

Tiger tail, a plastic-coated steel wire for heavy or sharp beads, will not cut or fray. With light beads it may kink and break.

Silk thread is strong and ideal for beads with finely-drilled holes, such as semi-precious beads. Either use it with a needle or stiffen the end with glue or nail varnish and thread through the beads.

The finest brass or copper wire for threading beads onto designs such as a perforated disc brooch.

0.6 mm, the most versatile wire for earrings and chokers.

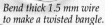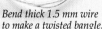

Bend thick 1.5 mm wire to make a twisted bangle.

Elastic thread is easy to use: simply thread on the beads and tie a reef knot.

Gold and silver elastic for added interest.

NEEDLES
Needles are used with silk and nylon thread for stringing beads and making knots.

Beading needle, fine and pliable, with a small eye.

Sharp, the most common type of needle.

Crewel needle with a long eye for embroidery silks.

Tapestry needle, blunt with a big eye, ideal for children.

Twist copper wire to make a small-eyed needle for tiny holes.

Laces Different thicknesses of cotton lace and leather are ideal for threading beads with larger holes.

FIXATIVES
Adhesives are used to stick flat-backed beads to findings and to set knots on all types of jewellery.

Superglue with a fine nozzle secures knots well.

Clear nail varnish is invaluable, but allow it to dry properly.

Ribbon Available in various sizes, ribbons look good sewn onto earring or brooch findings.

Shallow trays keep beads sorted while you work. Choose a tray with small compartments and a transparent lid to keep out dust.

Masking tape secures a necklace to stop beads escaping while you thread.

PLIERS
Four types of pliers are useful in jewellery making.

Round-nosed pliers with rounded ends are essential for forming loops as they give a rounded finish.

Snipe-nosed pliers, with round tips flattened on the inside, open rings and squeeze crimps. The most versatile pliers, they can also make loops.

Flat-nosed pliers squeeze crimps, close triangles, bend wire and hold jewellery steady while you work with the other hand.

Cutters snip wire cleanly and easily.

Scissors should have sharp, thin blades.

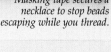

Earrings

Earrings made from beads, whether elaborate creations with many parts, or the simplest of drops, are generally made using the same principle: first thread the beads onto a headpin or an eyepin, then make a loop and attach it to your chosen earring fitting. All the earrings shown can be hung from fittings for pierced and unpierced ears; for heavier earrings, clips are best. Choose hypoallergenic fittings if your ears are sensitive.

INSTANT FITTINGS

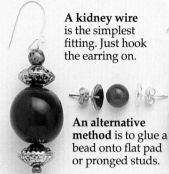

A kidney wire is the simplest fitting. Just hook the earring on.

An alternative method is to glue a bead onto flat pad or pronged studs.

Any fitting with a loop can be used to hang an earring.

Squeeze a triangle through a bead and hang from a hook.

USING A HEADPIN

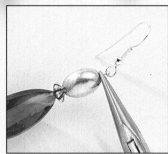

1 Thread the beads onto the pin, putting a smaller bead on first if the bottom bead has a large hole. Cut the wire, leaving about 6mm.

2 Twist a loop using round-nosed pliers. Pull gently towards you as you do so to keep the loop even.

3 Attach the loop on the pin to the loop on your earring fitting. Firmly squeeze together the loops with snipe-nosed pliers.

USING AN EYEPIN

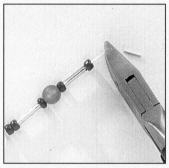
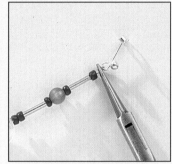

1 Open the loop on the eyepin with pliers. Thread on your bead or motif and tightly close up the loop.

2 Attach your chosen beads to the eyepin and cut the wire to fit your design, leaving 6mm to make a loop.

3 Attach the fitting and twist the top of the pin over tightly to close the loop.

VARIATIONS USING EYEPINS

Large pendant beads and other motifs can be attached by a triangle directly to the loop on the eyepin.

Two eyepins can be suspended from the same fitting if linked with a jump ring. Attach to the fitting loop as before.

A hoop is made from wire shaped like an eyepin. Thread beads onto the wire, form a loop at the end and attach to the loop at the base.

VARIATIONS USING HEADPINS AND EYEPINS

Link a headpin to the loop on an eyepin to make a long earring hang fluidly.

Hang 2 headpin drops from an earring finding on a ring. Ensure the beads nest neatly together.

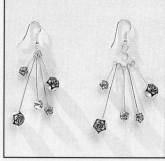

Attach a cluster of headpins to a jump ring, then hang from the loop on a fitting.

LOOPED WIRE EARRINGS

1 Thread beads onto eyepins. Cut off the excess and make a loop, leaving it slightly open. Make 3 sections on headpins.

2 Join several pins together by placing one loop inside another and squeezing tightly shut with flat-nosed pliers.

3 Attach the top loops of each length to a spacer bar. Add a ring to the loop on the spacer bar and hang from a fitting.

TASSEL EARRINGS

1 Leaving 10 cm of thread spare, thread up 7 strands. Knot them together near the beads.

2 Bend a headpin backwards and hook it through the knot. Then cut off the excess length.

3 Thread the pin through a cord cap. Cut off the excess and form a loop. Attach to a finding.

PERFORATED DISC EARRINGS

1 Using a needle, make a knot at the back of the disc and thread beads in and out to create a design.

2 When complete, knot the thread at the back of the disc. Cut off the excess and set the knots with nail varnish.

3 Clip on the perforated disc back by pressing down the claws with flat-nosed pliers.

Necklaces and bracelets

Making necklaces and bracelets is as simple as pushing thread through the hole in a bead, securing with a knot or crimp, attaching the clasp and putting on your creation. As far as technique is concerned, bracelets are simply short necklaces.

Page 116 shows all the techniques essential to fitting different types of fastener at the end of a necklace. Techniques for creating more advanced effects in the middle of a necklace or bracelet are featured on page 117.

KNOTTING ONTO A CLASP

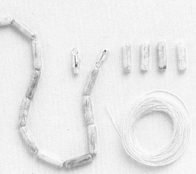

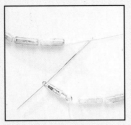

1 Passing the needle and thread through one clasp loop, make a knot and leave a tail. Set with nail varnish.

2 Thread the needle through the beads, and take it through the other loop on the clasp, then make a knot.

3 Thread the needle back through the last bead, or more if using smaller beads.

4 Knot between the beads. Cut the thread. Repeat steps 3 and 4 with the tail. Set both knots with nail varnish.

USING FRENCH CRIMPS

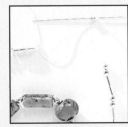

1 Pass a needle through 2 crimps, one loop on the clasp and back through the crimps.

2 Draw the crimps close to the clasp, leaving a tail, and squeeze them shut.

3 Thread on all the beads followed by 2 crimps and the clasp, as in steps 1 and 2.

4 Finish the ends by threading back through the last few beads, as above.

USING CALOTTE CRIMPS

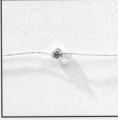

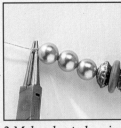

1 Tie a double knot near the end of the thread and then pull the knot tight.

2 Fit the knot into the crimp and squeeze shut with the thread coming out through the hole. Thread on the beads.

3 Make a knot, drawing it into the last bead with round-nosed plier tips. Squeeze a crimp over and cut off the ends.

4 Open the crimp loop, slip in the clasp loop and shut. At the other end attach a jump ring.

USING LACE END CRIMPS

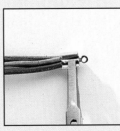

1 Place the thread (you can use one or more) inside the crimp.

2 Close one side of the crimp by pressing it with flat-nosed pliers.

3 Close the other side of the crimp using the same technique.

4 Open a jump ring and link it through the loops on the clasp and the crimp. Squeeze shut.

PINNING FOR A PENDANT EFFECT

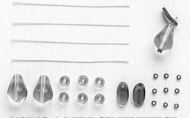

USING A WIRE CENTREPIECE

USING MORE THAN ONE STRAND

ATTACHING A MULTI-STRAND SECTION TO A SINGLE THREAD

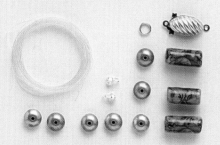

LOOPED WIRE TECHNIQUE

1 Thread the beads onto headpins. Cut off the extra pin, leaving about 6 mm.

2 Using round-nosed pliers, turn over the top of the pin to make a loop.

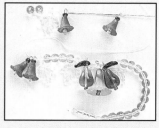

3 As you thread on the beads, thread the pins together to make clusters.

1 Make a loop in the wire with round-nosed pliers, as above, to create a stiff centrepiece.

2 Thread on all your beads, and leave enough wire to make a loop in the end.

3 Attach the wire loops at each end to crimps at the side of the necklace, as before.

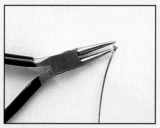

1 Knot together your strands, here 4, and squeeze a calotte over the knot.

2 Thread the 4 strands as if one. At key points separate the threads back into 4.

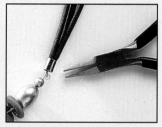

3 Pass the 4 strands through a bead and continue as if working with one. End with a calotte.

1 Make the single strand section, tie a knot and finish with a calotte crimp.

2 Squeeze a calotte onto 4 knotted strands, as above, then thread up the strands.

3 To join single and multi-strand pieces, open one calotte loop and press shut in the other.

1 Make a loop in the end of a headpin, then cut off the head.

2 Thread on beads, cut off the excess pin and make a loop, leaving it slightly open.

3 Connect the pins by squeezing one loop tightly into the next with pliers.

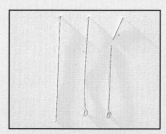

Brooches and pins

Brooches, lapel and hat pins, tie-pins and cuff links: all can be made with beads, some very simply and others, such as designs built up on a perforated disc, requiring more advanced techniques. As with all handmade pieces of fashion jewellery, you can create brooches and pins to match the colour scheme and the style of a particular outfit or accessory exactly.

LAPEL OR HAT PIN

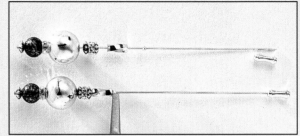

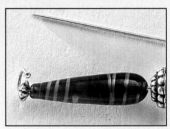

Remove the fastening at the end of the pin. Thread on the beads. To stop them slipping down, squeeze a French crimp up against the final bead with flat-nosed pliers.

LONG BROOCH

1 Take a lapel or hat pin and at the head bend 15 mm at right angles to the pin. Thread on beads to occupy slightly less than half the length of the pin.

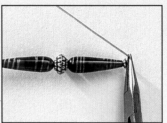

2 Bend the long end of the pin back behind the beads using snipe-nosed pliers.

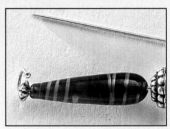

3 Make an angle in the head end of the pin to form a hook.

BOW BROOCH

1 Take your bow and secure the thread to the back by tying a knot in the end and sewing through the bow. You are now ready to start sewing on beads.

2 End each strand of beads with a stopper bead, threading back through the strand and through the bow each time.

3 Finish off by oversewing at the back of the bow and sew it onto a brooch pin through the holes in the top.

PERFORATED DISC BROOCH

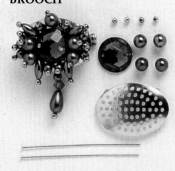

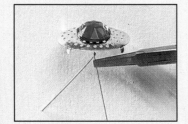

1 Fix a cabochon to the disc by threading headpins through the holes in the bead and the disc. Twist the pins at the back to secure. Cut off the extra length.

2 Make a knot at the back of the disc and sew the beads onto the front, taking the needle in and out through the holes and starting at the centre.

3 Once your design is complete, knot the thread at the back, dab glue onto each knot and fit the brooch back onto the disc by pressing shut the claws.

PIN BROOCH

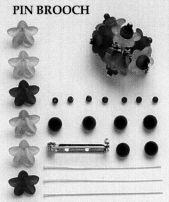

1 By pinning (see page 117), thread beads onto headpins. Leaving 6 mm, cut off the extra wire. Turn over to make a loop.

2 Thread all the pins onto a headpin and bend it slightly to secure them. Cut off the head.

3 Thread the headpin through a pin-back brooch fitting and twist the ends at the back to secure. Cut off the excess length.

FILIGREE BROOCH

1 Glue a flat-backed bead onto the centre of the filigree brooch piece. Leave until it has set.

2 Using fine brass wire, thread beads (larger ones first) onto the filigree. Weave the wire through the beads and the filigree back.

3 Secure the wire at the back of the brooch by twisting, then cut off any excess.

CUFF LINKS

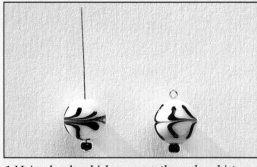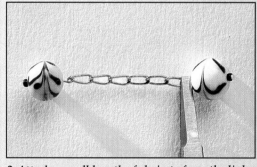

1 Using beads which can pass through a shirt button hole, thread each bead onto a headpin, cut off the excess length and form a loop in the end, leaving it slightly open.

2 Attach a small length of chain to form the links, by placing the last link at each end inside the loops attached to the beads. Squeeze the loops tightly shut with flat-nosed pliers.

TIE-PIN

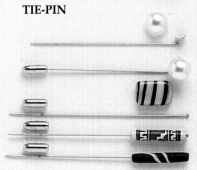

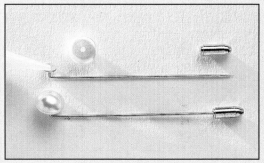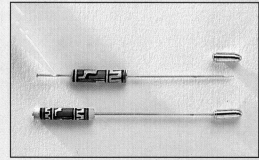

Glue a cabochon or other flat-backed bead onto a tie-pin base with a flat pad. Leave it to set.

Thread a bead onto a short hat or lapel pin and secure by dabbing some glue at the top of the pin.

Beading

Beading adds sparkle and originality to garments made from all but the finest fabrics. When beading, use embroidery silk, or a strong polyester thread for more sturdy fabrics, and a thin, pliable needle with a tiny eye. To bead small areas, work on a finished garment; if you are beading a whole fabric, bead before making it up to allow for fabric shrinkage.

Before starting to bead, design a template to follow.

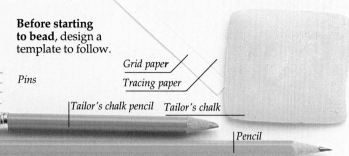

Pins
Grid paper
Tracing paper
Tailor's chalk pencil   Tailor's chalk
Pencil

PLANNING A DESIGN

1 Draw your pattern onto tracing paper. Bear in mind the size and shape of the beads when planning your design.

2 On the reverse side of the paper, trace over your design with tailor's chalk.

3 Turn the paper back to the right side, place it on the fabric and trace over the design with a pencil to transfer to the fabric.

For a symmetrical design, draw half the pattern on grid paper, fold corner to corner, then trace onto the other side of the paper.

SEWING ON A SINGLE BEAD
Always start by securing with two tiny stitches on the reverse.

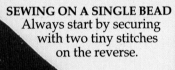

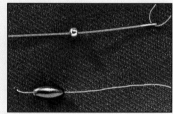

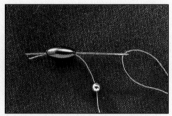

Come through to the front. Pick up a bead. A bead's width away pass to the back and overstitch.

1 If the hole in the bead is large, start as before, but pick up the bead and a small stopper bead.

2 Sew back through the first bead and secure on the reverse as before.

BACK STITCH
Back stitch is generally used to bead continuous rows.

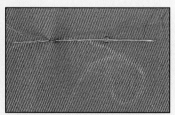

1 Using double thread, start by securing with 2 tiny stitches on the reverse of the fabric.

2 On the right side pick up a bead and make a small stitch back from right to left.

3 To add a bead, bring up the needle a stitch's length in front of the previous stitch.

COUCHING
Sew on ready-strung beads, turning the fabric as you work.

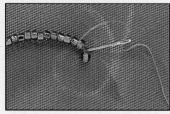

1 Fasten a double thread on the back and bring the needle up. Pick up a good number of beads.

2 Attach a new needle and thread near the start. Come up. Sew over the thread between beads 1 and 2.

3 Continue as before. Push each bead close to the one before and come up just in front of it.

LAZY STITCH
Lazy stitch allows you to cover large areas quickly.

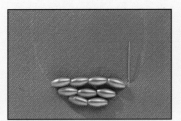

1 Work from one edge of the design across to the other, adding beads in rows.

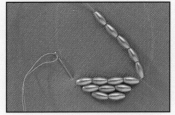

2 Pick up enough beads to fill each row. Sew through to the reverse when the thread is taut.

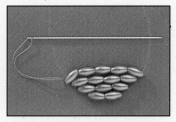

3 Come up near the last stitch, pick up more beads and pass to the reverse on the other edge.

FILLING STITCH
Use filling stitch to densely bead small areas.

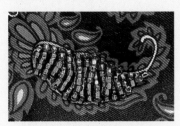

1 Starting at one end of the design, fill in the design with rows of beads.

2 Pick up precisely enough beads to cover each row. Pass to the reverse at the outer edge.

3 Bring the needle up again at the other edge, close to the last row of beads.

MAKING A LONG FRINGE
A long fringe looks good on scarves and wraps.

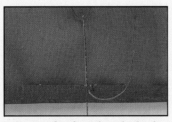

1 Secure the thread at the back of the hem and bring it out through the bottom.

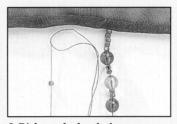

2 Pick up the beads for one section of fringe and pass through a small stopper bead.

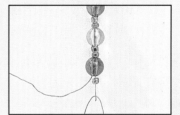

3 Thread back up through the beads and secure near your starting point as before.

MAKING A SCALLOPED FRINGE
The wavy effect of this fringe suits collars and sleeves.

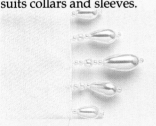

1 Secure the thread and pick up the beads and a stopper bead. Thread back through the beads.

2 When you reach the fabric, anchor the section with a small stitch and run along the hem.

3 Make a small stitch in the hem where you wish to start the next section and continue as before.

USING BEADING ON GARMENTS

To highlight a print, lay beads onto the fabric to establish the pattern, then sew them on using back stitch.

Add a border to the edge of a plain skirt. Each paisley motif on this skirt is beaded separately after the hem has been sewn.

Chiffon can be beaded with light beads and a very thin needle. If the fabric pulls, use an embroidery frame.

Before beading knitwear, either back the reverse of the area with fabric, or as here, appliqué onto the front to give a good base.

Caring for beads

Whether priceless heirlooms or cheap fashion jewellery all beads should be cared for correctly to look their best.

WEARING BEADS

Always put on your beads last, after dressing and using perfume, hair spray and cosmetics, to stop them from catching on garments or becoming coated by damaging substances. Never swim in your jewellery as chlorine, salt or immersion in water may damage the beads and weaken the thread.

DISPLAYING BEADS

You can display all but your most precious beads. Beads look very ornamental draped casually over a mirror on a dressing table or hung on the wall. A mannequin bedecked with ropes of beads looks beautiful displayed on the wall, on shelves or a plinth. Loose beads are decorative piled into attractive bowls and glass containers or spilling out of silk pouches.

CLEANING BEADS

To clean old beads, first find out what they are made from and use the method most appropriate for that type of bead. The most important adage is when in doubt do not clean them, as over-zealous cleaning can ruin lovely beads.

Ceramics and glass Clean the beads carefully in lukewarm soapy water and allow them to dry naturally.

Wood Examine the hole in the bead. If it is well polished and the rubbing of the thread has produced a patina, carefully dip the bead in soapy water. If the grain is coarse the wood will swell in water and spoil the bead. The best way to clean this type of bead is with a little saliva and a soft cloth, or use moistened baby wipes.

Pearls Leave all pearl beads to the experts to be cleaned. The nacre is very delicate and can be ruined by injudicious cleaning, so simply rub with a soft cloth.

Jet As with pearls, jet is best cleaned by rubbing with a soft cloth. Wear jet and pearls often as oil from the skin is beneficial and keeps the beads shiny.

Unknown substances If you do not know what the bead is made from be very careful. A gentle wipe with a damp cloth, drying with another soft cloth, will generally clean away any grime.

Solvents It is best not to use white spirit or other solvents to clean beads because they can destroy the beautiful surface of semi-precious stones and other natural products. Proprietary cleaners can also irritate the skin. Sometimes an antique bead gains in appeal from looking old and would be best cleaned with just a little 'spit and polish'.

STORING BEADS

Valuable beads and beaded fabrics especially should be stored in a suitable way.

Valuable necklaces are best kept separately in individual soft fabric pouches. They will tangle and scratch if stored together in glass or metal containers.

Porous semi-precious stones such as aquamarine, opal, rose quartz and turquoise should always be kept wrapped in acid-free tissue away from light and heat, which will fade the colour permanently.

Pearls are best worn frequently to keep the sheen bright, as dryness and lack of light or air can cause the surface to crack and disintegrate. Pearls are easily damaged by acid and grease, either from the skin or from cosmetics and perfumes. They should be frequently re-strung by a professional on silk thread.

Beaded textiles should be kept flat away from light, stuffed with pads of acid-free tissue to stop them from fading and to prevent the fibres from breaking down. If keeping your fabrics in wooden drawers, line these as well with acid-free tissue, but storage in acid-free cardboard boxes is better. Do not store fabrics in plastic because mould grows easily inside. Finally, check both beads and textiles regularly for possible damage.

Bead suppliers

Janet Coles Beads Limited
Perdiswell Cottage
Bilford Road
Worcester
WR3 8QA
For beads, findings, bead kits and jewellery-making service.

The Bead Shop
43 Neal Street
London WC2H 9PJ
For beads and findings, also wholesale and mail order service.

The Necklace Maker Workshop
259 Portobello Road
London W11 1LR
For antique and collectable beads and beadwork, findings and threads, commissions, repairs and threading tuition.

Ells and Farrier Limited
The Bead House
20 Princes Street
Hanover Square
London W1R 8PH
For beads, sequins, embroidery stones, findings and bead weaving equipment.

Creative Beadcraft Limited
Denmark Works
Sheepcote Dell Road
Beamond End
Near Amersham
Buckinghamshire HP7 0RX
Mail order division of Ells and Farrier for mail and telephone orders only.

Hobby Horse
11 Blue Boar Street
Oxford OX1 4EZ
For beads, findings and equipment for bead weaving.

Eaton's Shell Shop
30 Neal Street
London WC2H JPS
For shells and semi-precious stones.

Frontiers
39 Pembridge Road
London W11
For ethnic jewellery and semi-precious stones.

Index

Index

Acknowledgments

Authors' acknowledgments
We would very much like to thank all our friends and colleagues who so helped us in compiling the material for this book for their support, general encouragement and for providing us with invaluable clues, historical information and personal recollections. Our thanks especially to Jill Sudbury, Jan Kennedy and Carol Hames for their tremendous help in making samples for the themes and techniques sections and for their patient hours of beading. Thanks also to the whole team at Janet Coles Beads who assisted in many ways.

We are very grateful to Alby Merry, Stefany Tomalin, Wendy Turner Coates, Susan Wainwright, David Wainwright, Alex and Joss May, Kate Maclagan, Michelle Manguette, Sylvie Nordmann, Martin Russler, Anna Dickinson, Amina Ahmed, Luiven Rivas Sanchez and Joanna Spencer for lending us treasured beads from their private collections and for their wonderful encouragement.

To Alison MacDonnell for knotting, Elizabeth Turrell, Ann Baxter, Nicola Wade, Peter Ridley, David Halperin at Val d'Or Limited, 38 Hatton

Garden, London EC1, the Bead Shop, Hobby Horse, Swarovski, Meriden Beads, Ercole Moretti and Società Veneziana Conterie for lending us numerous beads and transparencies.

Thank you to Nicola Lesbirel at the Conran Shop, Fulham Road, London SW3; Victor Lamont and Ruth Paddy at Global Village, South Petherton, Somerset; Julie Wilson at Wilson and Gough, Draycott Avenue, London SW3; Patricia Wood at Mulberry Silks, Chipping Norton, Oxon; Nice Irma's, Goodge Street, London W1; Tower Ceramics, Parkway, London NW1 and Simon Buckland for kindly lending us props for photography.

To Daphne Razazan for her guidance when this book was but an idea and her tenacious help throughout its production. To Susannah Marriott, Tina Vaughan and Anne-Marie Bulat for their enthusiasm and hard work.

Finally to Andreas von Einsiedel, photographer, and John Golding who were so important in encouraging us at the embryonic stage of this project and for their very special contribution.

Dorling Kindersley would like to thank Jill Somerscales and Tanya Hines for editorial assistance; Karen Ward and Tracey Ward for design assistance; Hilary Bird for the index; Clive Reeve for research and design help; Tania Nott for modelling; Joanna Leevers, Nick Skinner, Simon Ardizzone, R. Holt and Company Limited, 98 Hatton Garden, London EC1 and Caithness Glass, Inveralmond, Perthshire, Scotland for supplying beads and props for photography.

Illustrators
Map pp. 16 - 17 Eugene Fleury
Calligraphy pp. 41 Bryn Walls
Illustration pp. 44 reproduced by courtesy of the Trustees of the British Museum
Engraving pp. 48 Società Venezia Conterie

Photographic credits
Photography by Andreas von Einsiedel. Jacket; p. 5; border pp. 10-11; Buddhist rosary, belt, trade beads pp. 18-19; finishes and coloured beads p. 15 by Stephen Oliver. Section openers by Dave King. Inset p. 10 Peter Brown; inset p. 14 Robert Budwig; Superbrilliant p. 15 Swarovski; inset p. 18 Angela Fisher.